Praise for *Lead*

"As a member of the Society of the Sacred Heart and as a chaired professor of management, I can say with assurance that this is a wonderfully deep, practically useful, stimulating and inspiring book. It provides coaching that is based on scholarly research, Ellen's reflection on her life experiences, and elegantly sketched examples that give advice we all can follow. It illustrates and encourages ongoing learning over a lifetime, rather than expecting us all to be perfect immediately in every encounter."

—JEAN M. BARTUNEK, Robert A. and Evelyn J. Ferris Chair
and Professor of Management and Organization,
Carroll School of Management, Boston College

"*Lead* is an essential part of your professional toolkit. Beautifully written, boldly comprehensive, and loaded with critical nuggets for navigating the professional world, Snee unpacks it all, from external biases to the limitations we place on ourselves—and, more importantly, provides great insights on what to do about it!"

—ROBIN L. MATLOCK, public and private board
member and former software executive

"Drawing from her research in psychology, Dr. Ellen Snee starts this highly actionable book for women leaders by asking the most fundamental question: *What do you want*? She leads the reader on a journey to find their own path to claiming power and authority from the inside out in the face of persistent structural barriers."

—CAROLINE SIMARD, PhD, Managing Director,
Stanford VMware Women's Leadership Innovation Lab

"Ellen's book is insightful and empowering. Her own experience from being a nun, corporate executive, and coach is unique in the business world. Ellen offers actionable advice on how to navigate systems and relationships and ultimately claim our authority in any situation; *Lead* is a must-read for aspiring women leaders!"

—BARBARA ADACHI, former National Managing Partner, Women's Initiative, Deloitte (retired) and President & Board Chair, International Women's Forum, Northern California

"A book that should be a graduation, promotion, and special occasion gift for every woman in business. Reading *Lead* is like having Ellen by your side—cheering on your efforts, sharing candid and relevant career stories, and providing practical end-of-chapter tools."

—JESSICA PARISI, President & CEO BTS North America

"*Lead* lays out a clear action plan to balance authority with leadership. But what gives this book its power are the stories about the women Snee has coached and led throughout her career. This book is a must for any woman seeking to claim authority while leading in today's world."

—THERESA KUSHNER, former Sr Vice President, Dell Technologies

"If you are ready to build your authority and use your power to effect change within your organization, this book is a must-read! Snee's wisdom, depth of experience, and commitment to women leaders shine through on every page. I recommend it highly."

—DENISE BROSSEAU, best-selling author of *Ready to Be a Thought Leader?*

"I finished *Lead* and absolutely loved it! The content, writing style, and examples make it a great piece of work. It will great be for any female leader, aspiring or already in a position of authority. It should be compulsory reading at business schools. I wish I'd had it thirty years ago!"

—SUSANNA HARKONEN, Founder and CEO, Innerwork

"As a woman leader, I honestly couldn't put the book down; I wanted to capture the nuggets in each chapter. I loved the actions/next steps at the end of each chapter—I like to set goals, so it was perfect for me."

—LAURA ORTMAN, President, Cologix, Inc.

"Reading *Lead* was like getting a live coaching session with actionable insights. It lit a fire inside me! The topics Ellen touches on are very relevant to women striving to lead and succeed in today's work environment."

—RASHMI GUPTA, CHRO, PRO Unlimited

"With *Lead*, Ellen Snee gives us a blueprint for leading and living in our power and influence by working with our inherent authority. Her coaching expertise shines through every page of this book, which is bound to help many women build a brighter future for themselves."

—JULIE ABRAMS, Founder and CEO of
How Women Lead and GP of How Women Invest

"As an advocate for technical women, I realize the importance of learning leadership skills, and *Lead* provides a powerful tool for all of us. Snee covers essential topics such as listening to your inner voice, catching success, creating executive presence, and demonstrating your authority, and I couldn't put the book down. The book will be an ongoing resource for many, and following its simple steps can lead to profound change."

—DR. TELLE WHITNEY, cofounder of the
Grace Hopper Conference and former CEO
of Anita Borg Institute

"*Lead* is a distillation of insights, stories, and suggested actions steps based on Dr. Snee's conversations and coaching experience with women executives. It integrates her field research and work experiences as a nun, an entrepreneur, an executive, and a coach—a must-read for women leaders."

—HOMA BAHRAMI, Professor, Haas School of Business,
University of California, Berkeley

"In *Lead*, Ellen achieves the near impossible balance of offering practical, spot-on advice combined with brilliant research-based insights. *Lead* is a playbook for successfully navigating the workplace."

—LORI NISHIURA MACKENZIE, cofounder of the
Stanford VMware Women's Leadership Innovation Lab
and Lead Strategist of Diversity, Equity, and Inclusion
at Stanford Graduate School of Business

Lead

Lead

HOW WOMEN IN CHARGE
CLAIM THEIR AUTHORITY

Ellen M. Snee, EdD

She Writes Press, a BookSparks imprint
A Division of SparkPointStudio, LLC.

Published 2021

Printed in the United States of America

Print ISBN: 978-1-64742-070-3
E-ISBN: 978-1-64742-146-5
Library of Congress Control Number: 2021908665

For information, address:
She Writes Press
1569 Solano Ave #546
Berkeley, CA 94707

She Writes Press is a division of SparkPoint Studio, LLC.

*To all women around the world
who claim their authority and Lead*

Contents

——

Introduction

—

This book originated in a cavernous classroom at the Harvard Kennedy School.

The sounds of holiday revelers on the streets slipped in as snow-dusted students opened the thick oak door. In the room, emotions were palpable above the chatter. This was the last night of a course on leadership and authority that had been like no other. Beyond the frameworks and theories presented, each encounter had functioned as a laboratory, designed to enable students to practice the leadership principles we had been taught. Our professor had urged us to push ourselves into the fray, to go to the "balcony," to gain a different perspective. We had tracked language to uncover its function as a trigger or uncover cues to underlying dynamics. We had learned to watch an "initial event" for insights into what would follow, and how the pressure in a group rose or exploded. We had been stretched to our limits, individually and as a group. But we had not yet addressed conclusions. How would this course come to an end? Would things be wrapped up? What might happen in this last session together?

As my mind wandered back over the semester, the professor entered our classroom, removed his coat, placed his papers on the podium, and, with the same calm he had demonstrated each week, launched the class by returning to his central theme: "Leadership

1

includes not only the task at hand," he began, "but the relational work within the group that is needed to accomplish—"

Before he could finish his sentence, a student in the front row asked with exasperation, "But what about the role of power?" I recognized him as a retired military officer from Pakistan. "I still don't understand why you don't talk more about power."

Before the professor could respond, a second man, someone who had repeatedly dominated class discussions, interrupted, "It's about how you *use* your power. If you convince everyone that you have the best idea, they will be happy to let you make the decision." He turned and looked around the class with a smug grin on his face, as if he had just played the winning hand in a poker game. But he was greeted with a low rumble in the room—a fatigue with his insistence that he knew more than anyone.

And so it continued: The bright young man from Beijing who, earlier in the semester, had questioned my ability to be a leader in our small group used that momentary pause to jump into the fray. "What about the *great man* theory of leadership? Isn't it true that some people are cut out to be leaders and others are not?" he asked.

The collective groan was louder this time and accompanied by comments about his condescending tone. No one seemed to take issue with his emphasis on *great man*, despite our repeated exchanges about gender during the semester.

With that, a tall, quiet man spoke up. "What the professor said is right. There is always relational work that gets in the way of accomplishing a group's task. The sooner we can *get that out of the way*, the faster we can get to the work to be done."

This time, the response included chatter from the women, who were losing patience and expressing our disbelief and frustration. All the work we had done seemed to have made no difference on many of our classmates. Our male colleagues were still eager to identify leadership with accomplishment, and relational work as something to "get out of the way." I couldn't believe how quickly the alpha males had reverted to the views and behaviors they had brought with them when the class began. Had they learned nothing in the past few months?

As I sat there watching it all play out, I recognized that I was feeling the same powerlessness that had driven me to take the course. My behavior was the same as when we had started. I apparently hadn't mastered the class either. Looking around the room, I made eye contact with Jessica, a young woman from Sweden. Her face was scrunched into an expression that shouted, *Really?* As our gazes connected and we did a simultaneous eye roll, I knew that I wasn't alone in my experience. She shared my incredulity. It seemed as though we might end where we had begun—each still approaching the "fray," or the work to be done, the same way we had before the semester had begun.

As I tried to make sense of this conundrum, my thoughts traveled back over the roller coaster semester. We had been given a novel toolbox of frameworks, language, and behaviors that had the potential to transform not only how we conceptualized leadership and authority but how we put those concepts into action. A family-systems therapist had helped us examine how our personal history impacted our exercise of these roles. We had worked in small and large groups, trying out new behaviors and giving each other immediate feedback. It had been excruciating and exhilarating at the same time.

As the recollections swirled and I tried to figure out what kept me from being more effective in situations like the dynamic in front of me, I kept returning to questions about authority, despite the fact that the course's emphasis had been on how to demonstrate leadership.

The professor's views of leadership rang true with my experiences working in all-female organizations. The women leaders I had known were able to adapt to the unknown and were committed to the relational work involved in holding a role of authority.

But as I left the classroom on that last night, I found myself repeatedly asking myself, *If I didn't like what was playing out, why didn't I do something about it? Why didn't I assert my own authority, enter the fray, and try to influence the dynamic?*

I had a new set of questions. What would it take to show authority in a situation where it was needed? How could I implement what I had learned in the course in a way that incorporated authority in the exercise of leadership? How might other women do that? I began to see that my questions about authority were linked to the reasons I had come to Harvard in the first place.

I was there to pursue a doctorate in women's psychological development—a pursuit sparked by my earlier work as a career counselor, where the literature was written by men and did not match the stories I heard from women I worked with. I had been a Catholic nun with the Religious of the Sacred Heart, an international order of educators committed to the education of girls and to social justice, for eighteen years and had considerable experience living and working in organizations where all the leaders were women. I had seen how women could be great leaders whether or not they held roles of formal authority. They could organize and mobilize individuals, teams, and organizations. They undertook the relational work of leadership with care and skill. The importance of leaders' listening to and connecting with others seemed obvious to me.

At the same time, the challenge to hold roles of authority in systems where the dominant models appeared more aligned with the use of power and control presented many challenges for women. Studies of women's leadership in the early 1990s, such as *The Female Advantage*, by Sally Helgesen, and the popular *Harvard Business Review* article "Ways Women Lead," by Judy B. Rosener, were still addressing how women acted differently than men. I wasn't interested in gender comparisons; I wanted to understand what worked for women in roles of authority.

Introduction

I had come to Harvard to work with Carol Gilligan, who had developed a research methodology focused on listening to women's and girls' voices. Her groundbreaking book *In a Different Voice* had, through its examination of interviews with women and girls, uncovered an alternative story of human experience, a different story of relationships, and thereby expanded our human understanding of developmental psychology. I hoped her research and methodology would enable me to design and develop a new framework for women's leadership development.

I began to see how the two fields that I was so eager to study—women's psychological development, and leadership and authority—actually came together. I was quite confident that the women I had known in roles of authority already understood the importance of the relational and reciprocal nature of leadership. But what I wanted to explore was how they thought about and navigated the *authority* that accompanied their leadership in organizations.

The theoretical foundation of my research would be women's psychological experience through the lens of developmental psychology. I would build my dissertation on the theory and research of Carol Gilligan and others at Harvard, as well as work done at Wellesley College by Jean Baker Miller and her colleagues, who were creating a model of psychotherapy for women. This book continues that work, additionally incorporating ideas from Deborah Tannen, Sheryl Sandberg, Brené Brown, and many others.

I am not saying that the lessons and insights found in these pages do not apply to men, but I am saying at the outset that that is not my objective. I am speaking to women, sharing knowledge gained from research and from my experience working with and listening to other women.

My insights are also infused with my rather unique experience of having lived and worked for eighteen years as a Catholic nun in an order of highly educated, talented, extraordinary women leaders. This experience allowed me to see what women leaders across the globe look and act like—a far cry from the stereotype of nuns seen in movies or on TV. These women have run multimillion-dollar organizations, have mobilized people across the world, and have dealt with the patriarchy of the papacy with grace and fortitude. I have witnessed firsthand the personal cost that a male power structure can exact on women leaders, the power of a united front, and how clarity about your goal can keep you focused on what really matters. This perspective and experience have informed this book, beginning with my emphasis on discerning one's deepest desires, continuing on to insights on the importance of forging relationships between and among women, and including the necessity of understanding the structures and systems within which we are embedded.

A few years after that tumultuous class, and shortly after graduating from Harvard with my newly minted doctorate in developmental psychology, I launched a boutique consulting firm, Fine Line Consulting, to work with Fortune 500 companies to advance and develop their top female talent. At the time, this was a relatively new offering and my colleagues thought I was crazy to be starting a business to work only for and with women—they saw it as the surest way to quickly go bust. I stuck to my conviction and passion to make a difference for women, and before long, Fine Line was thriving. I hired other consultants to join me, and we brought our work to the likes of Marriott, Goodyear, Avery Dennison, Charles Schwab, Motorola, Texas Instruments, Pfizer, and dozens more. We presented at major conferences, including the Conference Board, Linkage, and corporate and academic programs. We coached women globally, as well as nationally. And we saw our clients advance to C-suite roles, CEO positions, and boards of directors.

A decade later, when one of my clients offered me a position as VP of leadership and organizational development in a rising technology company, I exited Fine Line to take on the challenge of working as a leader in a role of authority *inside* a company. This included oversight of programs and processes for talent development; employee engagement; and a major business initiative to increase the recruitment, development, advancement, and retention of women. The years I spent working inside this company gave me additional insight into how to balance leadership and authority within a system. I learned firsthand how women can use their influence and power to mobilize the resources of a company to effect change both within their organization and on behalf of the broader community, through the creation of the company's foundation. I saw how courage and conviction can drive the exercise of authority powerfully and effectively.

Lead differs from other management and leadership books in a number of important ways. For starters, the locus of authority throughout is women's experience: personal, relational, and systemic. I encourage women to explore, understand, and trust their own experience even as I offer them suggestions and ideas for how to maximize their effectiveness within the structures and relationships of their roles. My recommendations come from a developmental model that argues we can always grow and improve. I reject all deficit models that suggest women don't have what it takes to provide leadership or exercise authority.

I have always been a bridge builder and have sought to connect the dots at work and in research. In this book, I have tried to bring to bear insights from both academic and popular writings in psychology, management, leadership, and trade fields. This is not a memoir, but it does draw heavily on personal stories and profiles of clients. My hope is that these vignettes powerfully illustrate key points as only stories can.

My intention in writing *Lead* was to avoid as much as possible the emphasis on gender comparisons that is a predominant factor in earlier works on women leaders. I am not arguing for an essentialist view of women, nor am I saying that all women act, lead, or hold authority in the same way. Nonetheless, in my three decades of working with women in roles of leadership and authority, I have found observable patterns in how they speak about their experiences. My goal is to distill and discuss these shared experiences so that they can be useful to other women.

I am not naive. I know that women's scope of power and influence is often severely limited and frequently impeded. We continue to marshal our energies to be seen, heard, and taken seriously. This is especially true for women of color. Yet I also believe in the energy and power that can be found when we work from the inside out to know what we want, strive to achieve it, and, together with other women, continue to speak truth to power. None of this is easy, but more of it is possible than we often realize. I have stood in awe at the women who have done the work, found their passion, pursued their desired path, and arrived at unexpected but glorious destinations.

Finally, I want to acknowledge the limitations of my knowledge of the experience of women of color. I have a long and deep academic knowledge of sexism, racism, and how they intersect. I also have lived and worked in racially and ethnically diverse communities as a nun. But none of that is the same as understanding firsthand the experience of women of color in the world of business. I am acutely aware of how my career has benefited from white privilege and how few of my clients have been women of color. These circumstances are in part a reflection of the small percentage of women of color who occupied senior roles in corporate America when I was running Fine Line or, more recently, in Silicon Valley. I am grateful for the women of color who have become my colleagues, mentors, and friends and who have helped me to think more critically about the intersection of race and gender in the world of business. Yet, as a white woman, I must be honest, transparent, and humble and acknowledge the limitations of what

Introduction

I can claim to know about nonwhite women's experiences with occupying roles of authority.

I have chosen to design this book as more of a dialogue than a declaration. My greatest success over the years has been in my one-to-one work with talented women who are eager to accelerate their careers, or who have reached the C-suite and feel as if they have entered a foreign land. I have sought to make the book as much like the coaching conversations I have held for twenty-five years: full of insights, examples, and stories, while also grounded in research. I hope that the reader feels as though we are in a conversation that is personal and that encourages her to apply the book to her own situation.

To help with this application, at the end of each chapter I have provided what I would call "homework" in my coaching practice: steps you can take to engage with the material by asking yourself questions, identifying opportunities for action, making a plan, and determining how to hold yourself accountable. Here is where knowledge becomes insight, where suggestion is owned, where wisdom is transferred.

The core framework for this book is one that emerged as I moved from academic research to the design and development of corporate leadership programs for women. I suddenly had to turn theory into praxis. I created a relational model built on women's psychological development—what I call Self-Others-Systems—which recognized that women are always in relationship to themselves, to others, and to the systems in which they live and work. Furthermore, all of these relationships intersect and interact in a dynamic fashion when someone exercises leadership in a role of authority. This framework provides the basic scaffolding for this book. The focus on relationship to self comes into play in chapters 1, 2, and 3; dimensions of one's relationship to others is addressed in chapters 4 and 5; and the exigencies of working within systems are explored in chapters 6, 7, and 8.

RELATIONSHIP TO SELF

This book starts with how we see ourselves, how we talk to ourselves, how we make decisions, how we frame the world. In chapter 1, I build on my strong conviction that each of us has an inner truth that is both accessible and trustworthy. I share from my experience as a nun how I learned to discern in community, a practice that has many contemporary counterparts. Today, years later, we see great interest in mindfulness and self-reflection, and the work of Malcolm Gladwell and others corroborates my belief in the reliability of intuition. While business data and metrics are essential, I believe that we also have an inner source of authority that can increase our ability to act and lead more effectively—by listening to our truth from the inside out.

In chapter 2, I discuss how to support and enable our inner authority by increasing our resilience. In addition to both the elements of and obstacles to resilience, I zero in on how our internal voices can often sabotage our resilience. This includes how we speak to ourselves, what we say, and the habitual negative mantras that play unconsciously in our heads. I show how these inner dialogues have enormous power to strengthen or undermine our authority as leaders.

In chapter 3, I take a special look at what happens when we are in a role of authority in relationship to other women. This chapter could be considered one about relationship either to self or to others. I have chosen to locate it under "self" because many of the dimensions of these dynamics have remained for a long time at unconscious and/or unspoken levels and are best addressed first at the individual level.

RELATIONSHIP TO OTHERS

Effective leadership in roles of authority depends on how you understand and manage relationships. Most management and leadership books expound on how to navigate the relational dimensions of work. I assume knowledge of those basics and choose to focus instead on particular challenges and issues that can be stumbling blocks for women.

In chapter 4, I address a topic that is more often raised about women than about men: "executive presence." This term has historically been used to describe the je ne sais quoi that a woman is perceived to lack and that could keep her from the top ranks of leadership. While executive presence may be something that you "know when you see it," society has shown unconscious bias in how the notion has impacted women's careers. It remains an important concept to be aware of. Above all, you want to find ways to increase your confidence and convey your inner authority effectively. Language can be a key tool in accomplishing this goal.

In chapter 5, I address the importance of a 360-degree perspective on relationship building within your organization. Beyond the relationships with your boss and other executives and the immediacy of your direct reports, relationships with your business partners and other executives in HR, legal, and finance are key to your effectiveness as a leader. Investing time and energy in these relationships isn't a nice "extra"—it is central to building an internal network for the effective exercise of authority when necessary.

RELATIONSHIP TO SYSTEMS

Early in my career, I came to recognize the impact that systems have on leaders. Company and cultural norms, the expectations that have accrued, and messages about what leadership and authority should look like have all had an enormous impact on women's careers. Today, we are keenly aware of how systemic racism and sexism, with their subsequent impacts on individuals and relationships, affect our collective history, culture, and social networks.

Too often in the past, women have tried to cope with these systemic dynamics alone by focusing on their individual competence and performance. In so doing, they have often failed to fully appreciate the impact that systems can and do have on our work and our lives. In chapters 6, 7, and 8, I address different ways in which we can heighten our awareness, increase our competence, and activate our effectiveness through actions that address systems, as well as individuals. I show the importance of initiating regular exchanges with your boss, demonstrating financial acumen, and constantly expanding how you are known not only in your company but in the broader communities to which you belong.

Chapter 6 addresses critical conversations to have about your own performance and career path. After a brief discussion of why many companies are moving away from traditional performance reviews, I suggest ways to structure conversations that will actually address the most relevant and useful dimensions of what I like to call "real work in real time." Perhaps more important, I try to show that performance alone, no matter how stellar, is often not sufficient for promotion. Certain skill sets require attention and opportunities to develop in order to demonstrate a person's readiness for more senior positions. These topics might structure a more successful career conversation.

Chapter 7 emphasizes the importance of developing financial acumen, rather than how to handle financial matters. It is an exhortation on the value of financial competence for nonfinance managers, as well as the importance of strong relationships with your finance business partners—insights that might not be new but too often are overlooked or forgotten.

Chapter 8 tackles the necessity of networking. Stressing the importance of "who knows you," rather than "who you know," I argue for using the strategic strengths I mentioned earlier to build webs of connection with individuals and organizations outside and beyond your own company. These relationships become increasingly important over the course of a career and are harder to build later than to build systematically over time.

Introduction

—

For as long as I can remember, I have wanted to write this book as a way to share the wisdom I have gained and the lessons I have learned with women I will likely never have the opportunity to meet. It has become my legacy, my way of paying it forward, my bucket list. Despite the volume of leadership books that come out each year, few are directed explicitly at women.

This book is different. This book is written for you.

While much has changed over these decades since I was first inspired to start down this road, much remains the same. My hope is that these pages contain insights that will be valuable to women who are seeking to accelerate their career, to hold roles of authority, or to thrive in the positions of authority they already occupy. And perhaps the book will offer some clarity to male allies who wish to better understand how to support and enable women to succeed as leaders.

I hope that this book, with its framework, examples, and insights, will enable you to accelerate your journey to the future you desire; strengthen your confidence in your competence; and help you find allies, mentors, and, above all, sponsors to speak about you. Today more than ever, the world needs your leadership to transform its structures and organizations. We need you to claim your authority and *lead*.

CHAPTER 1

—

Authorize from the Inside Out

In my mother's kitchen, on the wall above the table, hung a small wooden plaque with the words of the Serenity Prayer: "God, grant me the serenity to accept the things I cannot change, courage to change the things I can, and wisdom to know the difference." The plaque was one of the many religious items that my aunt Helen, a Catholic nun, gave to my family. My mother would glance at it when things went wrong, like when my father called to say he would be working late again. She mumbled the words to herself, an incantation against the challenges of her daily life. As I watched the message bring comfort to her, I instinctively memorized the words, even though I was still too young to understand fully what they meant. Years later, I would discover that this prayer that I had internalized was also the mantra of Alcoholics Anonymous, but for me its wisdom has always extended far beyond the challenges of sobriety.

While my mother turned to this simple message to accept what she couldn't change, I was always drawn to the second part:

"courage to change the things I can." Now I am convinced that we can change far more than we realize, whether that is our interactions and relationships with others, our feelings and attitudes, or our habits and behaviors. Once we recognize how our internal framing of life determines how we think, feel, and act, we can realize that we possess the power to influence and even alter the interpretive lens we use to view our experience. Our own "spin" on an encounter, our own replay of a conversation, can be a source of suffering, a distortion of what actually took place. But if we can pay attention to how we create that internal spin, we can find the courage and the power to change those things we can in fact change. This is where we begin to self-authorize.

Self-authorizing, where we name and claim our own power and authority, requires three steps: 1) recognize inner messages, especially our desires; 2) discern how we will achieve them; and 3) take action. The process starts within—by paying close attention to our inner prompts and voices. These are not mystical messages, but rather the marvelous connections our brain makes between the world around us and our thoughts and feelings. We harness these connections and gain insight through disciplined and attentive listening to our internal prompts.

RECOGNIZE

From my early childhood, I sensed that I innately knew some things, but I wasn't sure *how* I knew them. For instance, I knew when my mother was upset, despite her silence. I knew I was smart, even when my grades were poor. And I knew I didn't want to grow up and raise a family, although I didn't know why. I felt as though I had an inner voice that lived somewhere between my head and my heart and acted like an inner compass, providing direction, pointing to desire, and providing warnings. When I became a nun, I interpreted these messages as the "voice of God." Today I think of them as my interior source of authority.

The first time I actually vocalized my inner voice was the summer I turned twelve. It was a perfectly normal evening in our chaotic household of seven. A young priest from our parish who was a family friend had come for Wednesday night hot dogs and a game of Uno, our weekly family ritual. When it was time for Father Tom to leave, my devout father asked him to give us his blessing. We knelt, and he prayed over us. As Father Tom recited the Lord's Prayer, I suddenly felt an overwhelming sense of calling. I had a new awareness of what I wanted to be in life: a priest. When we stood, I was excited to share my epiphany with my family, sure that they would be as happy as I felt. I exclaimed to all, "When I grow up, I will become a priest!"

The silence was deafening. Then Father Tom said, "Uh, I think you mean you want to become a nun. Girls can't be ordained priests."

"No, I want to be a priest," I retorted, surprised and confused by his response. Looking back, I can see how naive I was at twelve not to have recognized the strict gender rules within the Catholic Church. But at that moment, I was driven by the deep desire I had uncovered. I wanted to be a priest—someone who could bring peace and healing to others, the way Father Tom had done with my family.

My mother looked at me with uncharacteristic blankness and then turned and walked to the kitchen. She still had four kids to get to bed and a kitchen to clean up. My heart sank. I thought wanting to be a priest was a good thing! Why didn't she say *something*? Surely, if my brother Jerry had said such a thing, she would have responded. Why was it okay for boys to have aspirations, but not girls?

That night, no one wanted to hear my truth. In fact, no one wanted to hear me speak. I knew what I wanted, what I was meant to be—perhaps even what God was calling me to become. But those closest to me did not acknowledge it. Instead, they simply but powerfully silenced me.

My family's dismissive response, however, did not diminish

my discovery of what I wanted, what I was called to be. The insight was undeniable, and it would be the indelible touchstone against which I would test other moments of recognition for the rest of my life. Beyond the insight itself was the realization that I could actually name and claim what I wanted, what called to me, even in the face of dismissal or opposition. I had discovered an inner voice that I had not known I possessed.

My experience is not novel. We all have access to an inner awareness of what we want, what we need, what we know in our hearts. But in today's world, where our senses are assaulted from every direction, it's hard to remember that a universe of knowledge lies within us, waiting to emerge. We forget what we know and lose sight of how to access our inner truth. Too often we turn to others—friends, mentors, coaches, therapists, and even social media—to find answers. These can be helpful resources and supports, but our real challenge is to unearth our inner wisdom.

One of the things I love about my work as a coach is enabling women to excavate their own knowledge and truth so they can recognize what they want and move forward with courage. Power is unleashed when a woman accesses her desire. She gains clarity and insight and new drive. Once she knows what she wants, the steps to get there are easier. Obstacles may remain, but her conviction propels her forward.

Coaching, for me, is about discernment, a process to uncover deep desires and identify the steps to make them real. This can be as straightforward as asking for your next promotion or requesting time off from work. Recognizing what you really want can take time, and sometimes it evolves only *over* time, but once discovered, the clarity demands action—even in the face of disappointment or setbacks, for, unfortunately, the world around you won't always do its part to support and encourage your pursuit. Yet my observation has been that once women "know what they know," they have the strength and determination to carry on.

One of my clients, Ivy, was a superstar at the New York pharmaceutical company where she worked. When I met her, she was already on the internal list of "high potentials," those who were viewed as future leaders and likely contenders for new opportunities. She seemed to have it all: an Ivy League doctorate, twenty years of experience, an outstanding business track record and glowing management reviews. Ivy served on community nonprofit boards and was a frequent speaker on issues of women's leadership. Her career goals were clear: She wanted to seize every opportunity to broaden her knowledge base and expand her responsibilities so that she would be ready for a CEO role in the next decade. She was passionate about the future and had been explicit with managers and executives about her aspirations.

Despite all this, as time went on, the leadership of her company moved at a painstakingly slow pace to advance Ivy. For inexplicable reasons, when new business opportunities appeared, her male colleagues—who had no more expertise or experience than she did—were chosen instead of her. At the same time, calls from recruiters increased. Eventually she began to take their calls; she wanted to see how she was viewed and valued elsewhere. When a promising offer came her way, she decided to go for it.

When Ivy met with her boss to tell him she was leaving, his reaction surprised her. He wanted twenty-four hours to come up with a counteroffer. Suddenly, her company seemed able to offer her something comparable: a promotion and the promise of additional advancement in the very near future. After weighing the two options, Ivy declined the external offer and stayed, hopeful that at last her career would take off.

Over the following three years, Ivy built one of the company's fastest-growing businesses. As the corporation grew through acquisitions, new opportunities to utilize her talent in a more senior role arose. Yet each time, her employer chose someone else, always making an excuse about why Ivy was not the right fit for that particular position, reminding her how highly she was valued, and assuring her that the right "match" would come along soon.

Eventually, Ivy recognized that she would not advance her business skills or her career where she was. When a trusted recruiter called with an opportunity to join a company bringing a new blockbuster drug to market, she decided to make the move. To her amazement, once again, her resignation triggered calls from members of the executive team encouraging her to stay. "Why would you leave?" they asked repeatedly. "You have a great future here," she heard over and over. But even then, no one mentioned a specific new role for her.

At that moment, Ivy realized they actually didn't know her or understand her career aspirations, despite her repeated requests for more responsibility and opportunity. The decision to leave was difficult—she loved the company and the people. But the truth was clear: She would not be able to achieve her career goals where she was. She took the new position—a move that was wildly successful and that put her on a clear track for a CEO role in the future.

Ivy is far from alone. Throughout my twenty-five-year career coaching women, I have repeatedly seen how women wait far longer than their male colleagues for key leadership roles. I have seen women given new positions with "interim" status while their company decides how to fill the role. This allows an employer to check out whether the woman will be successful, without putting all their support behind her, and to assess her performance, rather than place a bet on her potential. Far too often, I have also witnessed promises of future promotions or opportunities get conveniently forgotten until or unless the person in question is recruited away. Only then, when others are valuing and courting a woman, does her current employer ask what will make her stay.

Women can't rely on others to show us the ropes, to be on the lookout for opportunities on our behalf, or to promote us in discussions. We talk a lot about the need to have sponsors—individuals who will do such things for us—but the truth is that today, most women must remain proactive and responsible for their own career advancement. Be careful not to assume that good performance will lead to anything more than short-term rewards. Promotability requires a great deal more.

If you are working in a larger company, you need to ask yourself whether the executives are ensuring your career development or merely using your talent when problems arise. Is your advancement on par with that of equally talented male colleagues, or are you expected to jump through more hoops and demonstrate more patience? You must learn to recognize these patterns, know how to assess them, and address signs of inequity. In order to succeed, you must learn to be explicit about what you want and push back when you experience a discrepancy between how you and your male colleagues are treated—or, if you are a woman of color, differences between how you and your white colleagues are treated. You need to become savvy about systemic patterns of behavior within an organization and discern if and when change is possible.

For too long, we have assumed that concerns about hiring, promotion, and retention are best handled by human resources departments, despite the more recent emphasis in leadership training that the managers are responsible for the talent in organizations. Today we need to expand how we think about the recruitment and development of our employees as something we all share a role in and responsibility for. We all need to "take care" of such issues.

Talented women face multiple challenges. They have inner voices that say, *Be humble; don't talk about yourself too much* and that are reinforced by cultures that voice concerns about women who are seen as "ambitious." Women often face more layered expectations than what their male colleagues encounter—not just from men but also from other women. While different women encounter and respond to these expectations in different ways, they remain universal and are compounded by race, sexual identity, age, and class.

I am committed to changing culture and working to address unconscious bias in organizations. I have run programs for and initiated substantive change initiatives within companies. But I also believe that each one of us benefits from addressing the voices that burden us from within—those about ourselves, others, and organizations—for these have great power over us and can exert the greatest harm on a woman's sense of self-confidence and ambition. They also make us vulnerable to messages from others. That is why I am convinced that an ongoing process of discernment helps focus attention on both our inner dynamics and our external environment.

DISCERN

At many moments in my own life, I have struggled to determine the next steps in my career: my decision to become a nun, to enroll at Harvard, to leave religious life after eighteen years. In each case, it was a challenge to finally arrive at the realization of what I needed to do next.

As a nun, I learned a specific process for decision making, called discernment of spirits. Conceived of in the sixteenth century by Saint Ignatius of Loyola, the founder of the Jesuit Order of priests, it is designed to enable you to determine the path forward, or how to choose between different life options. This approach has become a spiritual foundation for many religious men and women around the world.

While Ignatius was recovering from serious war injuries, he observed how he experienced a range of emotions and noticed a correspondence between what he thought and how he felt. By tracking his emotions, he was able to determine which thoughts (or spirits) led to peace and which led to internal discord. While he attributed these thought patterns to the voice of God, what he describes in his writings is essentially a process of listening to your inner voices—however you understand them—and taking the path of action that brings the greatest sense of peace, which isn't always the proverbial path of least resistance.

Discernment shaped my years as a nun. You could say it was my modus operandi as it characterized how decisions were made—whether about where to live, the work I would do, or what I would study. The principles and practice of discernment gave me a language and a framework to understand experiences like that childhood moment when I knew I wanted to be a priest. I learned to recognize deep desires and how to pursue them.

This framework came to inform how I approached executive coaching with women. From the beginning, I wanted to hear and understand what a woman's inner truth was—what did she desire, what did she value, who did she want to become, what did she want to do? I believe that my role as a coach is to help women uncover and pursue these inner truths. Today, when I start coaching a new client, the first thing I try to understand is what she *wants*. This is the foundation and driver of all else. Rather than beginning with a series of 360-degree interviews with a client's colleagues, asking about her strengths and weaknesses, I focus on working from the inside out. I want to know what my client loves to do. I want to hear about experiences and events in the past that were successes in *her* eyes. I want to understand what brings her joy, what makes her happy, when she feels most alive. This is the path to identifying inner drives, passions, and desires.

Over the decades I have worked with clients, I have rarely met with a woman who knows what she wants at the beginning of our work together. The men I have coached are far more likely to have a concrete answer to the question, "What do you want to do next?" The list is endless: to have their boss's job, to be CEO in five years, to make enough money to retire at fifty. They have a specific goal in sight and typically know what it will take to get there. They have a plan, as well as a desire. With women, in contrast, I generally have to listen, probe, and push them to uncover their desires. Only after I've encouraged them to articulate their thoughts and identify their feelings do they gradually recognize that they *do* have an unspoken desire—a change in jobs, a promotion, a better relationship with a boss, or a seat at the table—and that the internal dialogues playing in their head are blocking the pursuit thereof.

Women are less likely to have a plan because we have not been encouraged to identify our desires. For generations, we have tried to balance our careers with family responsibilities, often feeling as if we are not doing a great job at either. We have not been encouraged to know what we want or to go after it. Instead, we have received messages about caring for others. Women have struggled with feelings of selfishness when we seek out something for ourselves.

Even when a woman knows what she wants to do in life, it can be hard for her to have the courage to tell the world, and even harder to take action toward achieving her goal. This is where coaches, mentors, friends, and family can be helpful.

Early in a woman's career, her desires typically focus on career advancement. When women enter our fifties, our plans for the future frequently change. We may have achieved considerable success in our career, but the work that got us there no longer sparks the energy or holds the interest it once provided. Women in law, accounting, or other technical fields can experience a pull to do something that has more meaning. Although this is often hard to define, it is an undeniable yearning to explore something bigger, broader, more impactful. The challenge is to clarify what that might look like and then determine how to identify and apply skills and experiences that are transferable. What will bring you joy?

Sophia is a client who went through this process. Her career was marked by success in consulting, running her own business, and then rising to CFO at a global technology company. Her only child was a few years from college, and her husband supported her career.

Personally and professionally, Sophia had become engaged in social and environmental causes over the years. Gradually, she felt a strong longing to "do more," and a certain boredom with finance. She began to consider a career shift but was nervous about the potentially serious financial consequences for her family.

Sophia continued at her "day job" but took every opportunity to meet and network with others who were engaged in the work she loved. She attended conferences and pursued an executive MBA program to sharpen her overall business skills and to expand her network. Her desire to make a change increased over the year that followed. Finally, she realized it was time to move beyond her current role. But first she explored if and how she could create a new initiative *within her company* that would address the direction she sought to go. She met with individual executives, worked on a strategic plan for her ideas, and finally presented to the executive team. They were interested in what Sophia had proposed, but ultimately decided that it was not the time—and she was not the person—to undertake the initiative.

When the door to pursuing this internal option closed, Sophia realized she needed to decide: Would she stay in her current job or leave to pursue her passion?

To help her assess the pros and cons of the two choices, I introduced her to the process of discernment of spirits that I had learned as a nun. I encouraged her to spend a few days imagining that she would leave to pursue the new venture. She should think about what life would be like. What might she do? Whom would she work with? What would her days and weeks be like? I urged her to immerse her thinking, feeling, and attention in this scenario and pay attention to how she felt, what thoughts and ideas occurred to her, and any dreams that emerged. I told her that she should make a careful record of all that she experienced and wondered. Then I coached her to do the same exercise again, this time imagining what it would be like to stay in her current job.

Sophia approached the exercise with her usual enthusiasm and discipline, and when we spoke the following week, she told me how she discovered in the discernment exercise that she must pursue her calling and passion whatever the risk or cost. Even though she loved the people she worked with and her position was both influential and lucrative, she was more disturbed by the idea of remaining where she was than by the idea of making a big change. She would resign and explore her next moves.

Sophia's story offers two big lessons for others. First, a new direction, calling, or deep desire emerges over time. As with the birth of a child, it takes care, nurturing, attending to the life within, and then a moment comes for the child to be born—a moment filled with both pain and exhilaration, a moment when everything about life changes forever. Second, Sophia's story illustrates how systems, organizations, companies, and even colleagues are rarely as open to bold and courageous new directions as we, and they, would like to think. New ideas may, with luck, get an audience or initial support, but an embrace of a major change is the product of years of influence, education, building executive support, and timing. These rarely align with the vision and drive of the early adapters. It can be a lonely, painful, confusing, and scary process to be on the forefront of an idea.

Sophia's experience also demonstrates the benefit of having another person to assist you with your discernment. You want someone who can offer guidance on how to process your options and who can listen carefully as you make your choice. That person will accompany you on your journey to know in both your heart and your head what you want and need to do. I've observed that this inner clarity becomes the strongest driver of the courage necessary to act.

ACT

Often the biggest challenge in a process of discernment is to *make the time* to clarify what you want. Uncertainty about the future—about a job, a relationship, a career step—brings with it confusion, discomfort, a gnawing sense that something is not right. By making time to face the uncertainty, taking the steps to discern the future, you can gain clarity, which will bring you a level of confidence even if the steps to be taken and the path to be followed is challenging or painful. But you can't ignore or underestimate the work and cost of putting a plan into action. Once I knew I would leave religious life, I had to locate the courage to take the next steps. Moving out on my own and finding a home, a job, and new friends took time, effort, and a great deal of psychological resilience.

I have observed that a similar process takes place for clients as they act on decisions they have arrived at through long and sometimes arduous internal discernment. Magdala is a good example. She was in her forties when we first met and had been working for a number of months at a national consulting firm. She was miserable. She had taken this job quickly when she left a smaller firm over repeated disputes with her boss. She was trying to determine whether she would stay at the new company or jump ship in hopes of finding something she enjoyed more.

I began by asking her one of my favorite questions—"What would you do if you won the lottery?"—by which, of course, I meant, "What you would do if you were absolutely free to do whatever you wish?"

At first, Magdala hesitated.

"I don't want to tell you, because you'll laugh," she said.

I was taken aback, since no client had ever said that to me before, but I assured her I would not, that I was genuinely curious to hear what her plans would be.

"I want to become a travel consultant for people who want highly curated international trips," she said, somewhat apologetically.

"Tell me more," I encouraged.

Her voice changed, and she began to describe the delight she took in planning unusual voyages. "Right now, I'm organizing a family trip to Italy and have arranged a high-speed drive through Rome in Fiat cars that my son and husband will just love!" She clearly had more passion for this avocation than for her current work, but it wasn't clear to me how to make this dream activity something that could support her family.

To explore how Magdala might get from here to there, I asked her to tell me about previous work experiences where she had succeeded and thrived. We examined the elements of those jobs that contributed to her success and arrived at a long list that included her love of managing a team, her intellectual curiosity, and how much she relished opportunities to be creative and original in business solutions. Despite its appeal, a job in the travel industry addressed only a few of her many strengths and passions.

Next, we examined Magdala's current job to determine what exactly was frustrating her so much.

"I hate selling product," she said with disgust. "When I took the job, I understood that I would be involved in strategy and operations, which is a great match for me. But after the first month, my boss was replaced, and the new guy wants me to be out selling, when I really just want to get back to strategy and working with teams."

I let the emotion settle before responding. "Let's talk about what you love to do—the strategy and operations."

When her eyes lit up, I knew I had struck where positive energy existed for her. She talked about previous successes and what she had envisioned doing at her current company.

"What if you spent some time in the next two weeks exploring how you might find a different role within this company that's a better match for your skills?" I suggested. "I'd also like you to start looking online for jobs that excite you—no matter where they are—so you can begin to identify more clearly what types attract you. These could be operational roles in other companies, especially those that have a reputation for valuing teamwork and encouraging creativity and independent thinking." I was trying to empower her to identify what she *was* attracted to, as a way forward and a counterforce to the negative pull of her current frustration and despair.

When we met two weeks later, Magdala was like a new person. She had found a company with brilliant people on its leadership team and that was local to boot. She had applied and was waiting for the interview process. The following week, she called to say she had been invited in to interview and had found the process extensive but exhilarating. Each conversation reminded her of how much she loved thorny problems and working with smart people who appreciated creative solutions. It appeared to be a perfect match in terms of people, culture, work, and mission. As she waited to hear the results (she was one of two finalists), we spoke about all the benefits that she had gotten from the experience, no matter the outcome.

Magdala didn't get the job—instead, a top executive from a Fortune 50 company was hired to fill the position. Her disappointment when she found out was enormous, but she also recognized that she had gained insight and direction from the experience. The process had enabled her to see that she was unhappy in consulting and needed to make a career shift. After a careful review of her finances, she determined that she could take a year or more off to explore her next career move.

She could also see that she had gained insight, clarity, and focus from the process of reflection, exploration, and examination that she had engaged in. She now had a much clearer picture of what she didn't want, including a travel company. She decided to take some time off to spend with her family, travel, and determine what she would do next. She started to plan the next amazing trip with her family and some home renovations that she had wanted to do and now had the time to oversee.

To maximize our internal authority, we must first identify what we want, discern how to make it happen, and take action to achieve our deep desires. I have watched with pleasure and awe as clients like Magdala have embraced the work that needs to be done. This does not always immediately result in their landing a dream job or finally getting that promotion they've been waiting on, but time and time again I've seen that when my clients do the work to identify what they want, they move forward to achieve amazing outcomes. Ultimately, they engage their hearts, minds, and wills and employ discipline, determination, and courage to "change the things that can be changed."

Chapter 1: Authorize from the Inside Out

Summary

- Pay attention to your inner dialogues.
- Distinguish empowering voices from your inner critic.
- Engage a trusted advisor to help you gain clarity and discern your emerging truth.
- Incorporate these insights into your leadership decisions, actions, and behaviors.

Do the Work

Learn:

- Develop a writing practice to track your inner dialogues.
- Notice your inner dialogues before, during, and after meetings. What do they sound like? What feelings are attached to them? What is your response? Reflect on them at the end of the day.
- Catch successes. What is your inner dialogue when something good happens? How do you reinforce success, whether big or small? Set a goal, and claim one success at the end of each day.
- Identify a specific inner critic you want to change. Identify when and where this voice occurs. How could you change the dialogue?

Engage:

- Find a listening partner who can provide feedback to your reflections.
- Gain different perspectives from a spouse or partner, a trusted friend, a mentor or coach.
- Determine *who* is the right person to ask.
- Consider the frequency, focus, and structure of your meetings.

- Identify your goals and how you will measure progress.

Articulate:
- Create a realistic plan each month.
- Focus on a particular inner dialogue that feels negative.
- Amplify moments of success.
- Apply what you know about learning a language, a new sport, or a musical instrument.

Do it:
- I will begin a writing practice by doing _____ starting _____.
- I will engage _____ as a listening partner. Together we will focus on _____.
- In the next [specify time period], I will work on the following behavior: _____.

CHAPTER 2

Develop Internal Resilience

To exercise authority requires resilience, the ineffable capacity to meet challenges and persist, to bounce back even when you get knocked down. I am writing this book during the COVID-19 pandemic—a time when leaders and employees, parents and teachers, and above all essential workers have recognized the need for resilience as they struggle with the new challenges of working remotely, sheltering in place, and facing an uncertain future. We all are learning to trust ourselves, solve problems, and endure together. While resilience seems particularly important during the pandemic, it is equally essential in the daily life of women in roles of authority, albeit in different ways in "ordinary times."

The good news is that resilience can be developed. Don't assume that some people are born this way and you are not. Instead, recognize that you can develop and hone resilience in and through the daily challenges and opportunities life brings to you. Think of the give-and-take of interactions with other people, like the kneading of bread. Let me explain.

Once a year, for Saint Patrick's Day, I make Irish soda bread using an ancient family recipe. I learned from my mother that the secret to a light bread lies in the delicate balance between a light touch when you're pushing the dough out and a quick, firm touch when you pull it back into a ball while kneading. I've never understood the physics of how this lets air into the dough and helps it to rise, but I do recognize that, as with so many experiences in life, the mixture of contrasts makes the magic.

Kneading dough is an apt metaphor for how a mixture of love and heartache, triumph and defeat, transforms our lives. We learn over a lifetime how to let our hearts be tenderized by pain and love and to let our will become strengthened by our response to the challenges that we encounter. The secret is a light touch and quick, firm resolve.

Our best models of resilience can be found close to home: women who struggle every day to balance family, work, community, and self. The demands of others at home, at work, and elsewhere push women to build resilience in even the best of times. Too often, however, most of us don't recognize how our resilience is developing amid the desperate hustle to get things done. This strength could become a greater asset if we could recognize and appreciate our power to persist. A resilience that is consciously chosen, carefully kneaded, will sustain women in authority at work and at home.

ELEMENTS OF RESILIENCE

Researchers tell us that five elements contribute to resilience: goal setting, taking action, mindset, a hopeful attitude, and self-concept. The first two—goal setting and taking action—are familiar activities to anyone who has worked in a company or organization. The latter three—mindset, a hopeful attitude, and self-concept—have gained momentum more recently in the business world. These skills—previously seen as "soft skills"—are now valued far more than they were in the past. Just as a body requires multiple systems (nervous, skeletal, circulatory, etc.) to work together, the same is true for resilience. Resilience is achieved when these five elements are implemented seamlessly and deliberately. Let's take a look at them one at a time.

Goal Setting

Most work environments make a religion of goal setting. This approach is based on the premise that you manage what you measure. SMART (specific, measurable, achievable, relevant, and time-based) goals are one popular approach for tracking progress.

Goal setting can drive teams, organizations, and companies, but I'll confess that I have never been a big fan of this approach. My skepticism stems from the inordinate amount of time and energy these processes consume and how often goals are set aside until quarterly or annual reviews. While goal setting can generate important conversations about business needs, the rigidity of formal goal-setting processes can also lock in direction, objectives, and expectations and fail to allow for the unexpected, the brilliant idea, or the solution not within the scope of objectives previously established.

My contrarian view on goal setting arises from decades of coaching talented women executives. I have watched in wonder when these women uncover and deliver *unexpected and surprising* outcomes that go far beyond the realm of their goals. These outcomes arise from creative, committed work and curiosity. Had they focused only on the goals that they were committed to delivering, great value would have been lost.

All this said, I've also worked within plenty of company cultures where goal setting is important. For example, when I was engaged to do coaching at a major tech firm in the early '90s, it had an elaborate process designed for coaches, one that involved goal setting, 360-degree interviews, and monthly updates on progress toward goals. I was happy to comply. I do believe in corporate processes as a tool to manage major initiatives.

However, at the beginning of a coaching engagement, I also say to a client and/or her manager that the greatest outcomes in coaching usually can't be seen or anticipated. They inevitably occur as the individual gains new insights into herself, her behavior, and her interactions with others. The ongoing feedback and guidance that coaching provides in turn enable the client to turn insights into behavioral change. The most important elements of successful growth are the desire to learn and the willingness to change, not the goals that are set.

Taking Action

In 2018, 244 women ran for Congress or for governorship positions. They were diverse in age, race, country of origin, occupation, and marital and parental status, and their political stances were equally varied. Many of these women were new to politics, driven to run by a passion for a particular issue: health care, Native American concerns, education. Several were veterans entering politics as a way to continue to serve. Women who never saw themselves as politicians were so impassioned by the state of government or a concern for women's health, children's education, or health insurance for all that they were willing to take action. Politics for them was truly personal. They stepped up to make a difference, to take action, to change the status quo on behalf of others.

I find inspiration and encouragement in these women. They remind me that often the path to unexpected but important action lies in one's inner passion. In 1995, after I graduated from Harvard, I saw few opportunities to work primarily on the advancement of women, and that was when I decided to launch Fine Line Consulting. People told me I was crazy: "Companies will never hire you," they told me. "You won't get enough work if you serve only women," others said. I knew nothing about running a business, but

I had a deep passion for making a difference for women. When I was a nun, our focus was on the education of young girls—a mission to do the work we did "for the sake of a single child." When I left the convent and finished my doctorate in women's development, that mission morphed into "for the sake of a single woman." My commitment to continue pursuing this goal enabled me to push into unknown waters and then learn how to swim.

In the years since, I have witnessed women labor over detailed plans for businesses and ventures. This is necessary but not sufficient on its own. Even with "perfect" plans, you still have to be willing to dive in and drive. Go for it, and you'll figure it out along the way. The women who actually *enjoy* their success are those who are clear on what their burning desire is, the reason for their direction, and what they must do to realize their desire. They know how they will measure success and can enjoy the steps along the path.

Mindset

We all bring a certain point of view to our work, but some people have a set of beliefs that are intractable. I once had a client, Myra, who was seeking a new job. Myra was convinced that she would fail whenever she applied for a new position or project. *The boss doesn't like me* or *Someone else is pushing for the position* were thoughts that colored her approach to any interview. It was painful to watch how her attitude impacted her career. I would coach Myra on her language, her presentation skills, and how to emphasize her experience and expertise. We would role-play the anticipated interaction. Yet when she entered an interview, Myra's previous assumptions would inform her performance, much to her detriment. The saddest part was that she was unable or unwilling to see her own framework and how it impacted her life.

A tool called Five Dynamics enables individuals and team members to see how they approach different stages of a project: explore (strategize, imagine options), engage (excite and mobilize others around the idea), examine (analyze the pros and cons), execute (make it happen), and evaluate (assess for success and satisfaction). Five Dynamics can help a team to see exactly where in a project each individual is at her best so she can use her strengths most effectively.

When I was at the Silicon Valley tech company VMware, my global leadership development team used Five Dynamics to help us work together more effectively. The report that the tool generated showed that I was off the charts in the "explore" category. That meant I could spend a tremendous amount of time strategizing about and presenting new ideas. There were two individuals who were more focused on "examine" and "execute," and it helped them to know they could put a halt to my brainstorming when it became excessive. I also learned that I could count on them to ensure that the ideas we generated as a team would be executed carefully and effectively.

Another popular tool is the Myers-Briggs personality profile. It fosters greater communication and collaboration by identifying team members' preferred mode of learning, processing, and decision making. For example, the first distinction is between introversion and extroversion. Myers-Briggs essentially contrasts them by explaining that an extrovert speaks to think, while an introvert thinks to speak. Knowledge of this difference is critical for team meetings. A leader needs to make sure she hears from the introverts despite their silence, since often they have thought through what they will suggest but have a hard time interrupting an extrovert.

Whatever tool a team uses, the purpose shouldn't be just to discover interesting facts about each other—it should be to uncover mindsets that can either help or hinder getting work done.

Hope

Hope is the scaffold for building resilience. Hope is the heart pumping blood to the brain. Without hope, resilience wanes. I learned this lesson in 2002, when I moved to California. After 9/11, my consulting practice had lost a lot of clients; companies had cut business travel for employees and especially for consultants. This circumstance gave me an opportunity to reevaluate what I wanted to do and where I wanted to be in the next chapter of my life. I shut down Fine Line Consulting and moved to California in hopes of starting over far from the gray skies and snowy winters of Boston. I had learned from 9/11 that life is short and unpredictable, and the one thing I knew was that I wanted to live where there was sun.

However, when I got to California, I was suddenly alone, without colleagues, clients, or easy access to friends. I tried to develop a consulting practice but didn't have the contacts to land company contracts. I became seriously depressed. This state of being and mind did not help to land any work, and that put my financial future in great jeopardy. As I lost hope, I found it harder to reach out to contacts or even to friends. My depression increased so much that at one point I took a trip to Boston to say goodbye, convinced that I would commit suicide upon my return to California.

Ultimately, it was only the intervention of a dear friend that stopped me from going past the point of no return. She recognized that my continual crying, my difficulty in focusing on work, and my loss of interest in seeing friends were serious. She got me in touch with a doctor who prescribed antidepressants and a therapist who helped me rebuild a sense of hope for the future.

I see now how my loss of hope during that time led to a loss of resilience. When I was in that state of mind, everything that happened felt cataclysmic. Yet once I was balanced medically and psychologically, I could resume work and build up resilience. Ultimately, I recreated my consulting practice, met the man who became my husband, and began working for VMware.

The loss of hope is often not as dramatic or traumatic as was that moment in my life, nor is hope the same as optimism. Rather, it is the confident expectation that what we do today will make a difference. This attitude fuels resilience and enables us to overcome challenges that might otherwise deplete us.

Hope is also magnified in and through community when we work together toward a shared goal. We see this phenomenon unfold within business teams driving to bring a product to market, and we see it in social movements seeking justice. A community, large or small, creates for its members a holding environment where each is enabled to carry on, even when individuals may feel as if hope is lost.

Self-Concept

Finally, resilience requires a positive view of oneself. We may frequently overlook how our self-concept impacts our activities and success. We fail to recognize the constant assessment process that takes place silently but pervasively somewhere in the back of our minds. Resilience requires us to view ourselves as people with power and control. This means that we have to find ways to manage our self-criticism. We need an inner lens that allows us to see a stronger and more confident self. Instead of our habitual self-criticism and even, at times, self-sabotage, we want to focus on the vision we have for who we want to be in the future. This vision of ourselves draws on deep beliefs: *Yes, I can become that person* and *Yes, I can accomplish my wildest dreams.* We need to build *confidence in our competence.* In this way, we can begin to manage the negative voices that pop up in our heads by depriving them of the oxygen of attention. They are drowned out by the new images and voices we have introduced and amplified. Our self-concept is strengthened by our deliberate determination to view ourselves in a new light.

Sometimes a client will admit to me that she doesn't *feel* confident. Rather than trying to convince her she *should* feel confident or what she could do to feel that way, I have found that a radically different approach is more successful. First, I remind her that

Shakespeare was right when he said, "All the world's a stage, And all the men and women merely players." Then I continue to point out that talented actors assume dramatically different characters and work hard to make them believable. This often requires that they think their way into the role—imagining how the character would behave or interact with others, for example. Their focus is on the work—to understand and portray the character, not their own feelings or level of confidence.

We too play a role when we take on a position of authority. Like good actors, we must invest time and energyto grasp that role and play it fully. Acting with authority sometimes means assuming the role even if it doesn't feel comfortable. The goal is to convey to others that you can and will set direction, provide protection, and make decisions. If you keep your eyes on the work to be done and the people who are doing it, you will not have the time or energy to worry about how you feel about yourself as a leader. Your self-concept will take shape in relation to what you have committed to deliver.

Over time, you will find that as your competence grows, so will your confidence. And when all else fails, I have also been known to say, "Comfort is highly overrated."

OBSTACLES TO RESILIENCE

Resilience grows with time, but not everything we think, feel, and do contributes to its development. Certain attitudes, mindsets, and feelings can impede or block its growth. I have seen three in particular that hinder women's success: extreme expectations of themselves, fear of failure, and internal voices. These factors are all closely related but worth considering as distinct dynamics that can thwart our desire to become resilient.

Extreme Expectations

I've found time and again that women are unaware of how ridiculously high their expectations of themselves are. I tell clients, "Cut back to 100 percent of what you expect to achieve, instead of 150 percent. You will still be 15 percent or more ahead of your male colleagues." It's a joke—but only sort of.

Women sometimes expect so much of themselves that no matter how well they do, they are afraid it's not good enough. They start with the assumption that they must deliver A-plus work all the time. Stanford psychology professor Carol Dweck, in her book *Mindset*, suggests that this is the aftermath of stellar performance in school. Women continue the work ethic that brought them to a role of authority, assuming that performance will lead to career advancement. Anything less than stellar performance causes anxiety.

The world of work, however, does not function the way school does. Career advancement is rarely a straight line marked by A-plus reviews. It often has unexpected twists and turns that require more than strong performance credentials. Opportunities arise that require you to acknowledge and accentuate your *potential*, as well as your performance, in your self-concept and presentation. Applying for a new position is a critical opportunity to do this.

While we know hiring processes are often biased, I have been dismayed by how often women themselves self-select out of a position for which they are well suited. In fact, researchers have found a dramatic gender difference in approaches to applying for a new job: Men apply for a job when they meet only 60 percent of the listed qualifications; women apply only if they meet 100 percent of them.

I have two stories that bear out this trend—one very public and one closer to home. When she speaks on stages across the country, Ginni Rometty, former chair and CEO of IBM, often shares a story about an experience from early in her career when she worked for a senior executive. One day he came to tell her he was leaving and that she would be his replacement. However, she did not share his excitement about the news. Her account of what happened that she shared at Northwestern University's 2015 Commencement address is quite telling:

> I looked at him and I said, Tsk, it's too early. I'm not ready. Just give me a few more years and [I'll] be ready for this. I need to go home and I need to go sleep on that. Well, that evening, my husband sat and listened patiently to my story, like he always does. And then he looked at me and he said one thing. He said, Do you think a man would have answered the question that way? He said, I know you. In six months, you'll be ready for something else. And you know what? He was right. And I went in the next day and I took that job.

We all need a person in our life like Ginni Rometty's husband. We all need someone who will challenge us when we underestimate our ability or fail to acknowledge our deepest desires. Over the years, I have had the good fortune of being that person to a number of friends and clients, one of whom, Lynne, found herself in a situation that paralleled Rometty's experience.

Lynne was a talented executive at a software company. She was considered high potential, and her name had appeared frequently in succession planning discussions. When I learned that her boss was unexpectedly leaving his position to go to another company, I immediately reached out to Lynne to see what her plans were. Over lunch, I asked her if she had let the CEO know she was interested in the position. "Oh, no," she said. "The timing is all wrong. I haven't run a large enough organization. I think I need to go be CMO of a smaller company and then come back."

I reacted less patiently than Rometty's husband had. A bit exasperated, I pushed Lynne to reconsider. I encouraged her to at least go through the interview process. That alone was a valuable opportunity. She would have a chance to meet with each member of the executive team to discuss her track record, her desire and vision for the organization, and her career aspirations. I was confident that she would find strong support from colleagues across the company, and I encouraged her to speak to some of her male peers and get their opinions.

It came as no surprise to me when, the following week, Lynne told me that her male colleagues had all said she would be crazy if she did not apply, and she had decided they were right. The process was long and tedious, but eventually she was promoted to the C-suite position. I can still remember her call to tell me the good news. Shock and surprise were mixed with exuberant delight. Only later did we both realize how close she had come to missing this opportunity by not "going for it." Today, Lynne tells other women her story of how I "kicked her in the butt" and how that made all the difference.

We need to be butt kickers for each other. We all need to be nudged to follow our dreams and take the risks that sometimes requires. As Rometty says, "Growth and comfort never coexist."

A female job candidate also needs a "cheering section" of friends, family, and colleagues to keep reminding her to say, "Yes, I can! Yes, I can!" Over the years, I have watched women gain positions they never expected. For each one, it took the support of others to help develop the mindset that she *could* do it and to let herself feel hope that she *would* do it, and a shift in self-concept to see that she *should* do it—i.e., go for the job. But we also need to internalize this desire and passion to "go for it."

When Kamala Harris was nominated as the Democratic vice-presidential candidate in 2020, it sparked a discussion about ambition in women. Research has repeatedly shown that while ambition is typically viewed positively in men, historically it has not been seen favorably when exhibited by women. This has often led to an unconscious hesitation to name and claim career ambition or success. Today, however, we see women trying to change that. In her book *Ambition Is Not a Dirty Word*, Debra Condren suggests eight Ambitious Rules: "Take credit, deflect detractors, handle confrontation. Be brave and be bold. Pursue your dreams and hold your head high. Go for your dreams." These are all behaviors that start with how we think and feel about our abilities and desires. They are all within our capacity to enact.

Fear of Failure

For women in large organizations, their fear of failure is often tied to worries that they won't meet the expectations of their boss or the criteria for advancement. For women entrepreneurs, fear of failure isn't about pleasing a boss or applying for a new position. It is much closer to home: Your every action impacts not only you but your business too. Failure can be even more frightening, since it is so personal: You fear that if *you* fail, you will take down your business and everyone connected to it. This can include failing to get enough accounts, make enough sales, manage resources effectively, hire the right employees, and know when to move people on. Since so much of the business actually *does* ride on you, the fear can become overwhelming and even paralyzing. Whatever your circumstances, even if you can't silence this fear, you must, at a minimum, learn to manage its nagging messages that you aren't doing enough, or that you might be failing others.

One way to address the fear-of-failure voice in your head is to find a support system of other women who understand your experience and can challenge you to forge ahead, despite the annoying voice you may be hearing. Women who are business owners can find and join a women's entrepreneur circle, such as a CEO group like the one I was part of while I ran Fine Line in Boston. The monthly meeting of a small group of women running vastly different businesses provided opportunities for feedback, a chance to learn from other women, and the support of others who were in my same situation. Today, one of the largest groups providing this kind of support is LeanIn.org. Its website reports that it has more than 43,000 Lean In Circles in more than 170 countries, and new ones beginning every day. This kind of external resource can help you gain perspective, see new directions, and, above all, get a reality check on how things are actually going. Today, social media has made it possible for many groups to form by industry, geography, interest, or level of responsibility. There is no reason not to locate such a support group for yourself.

You might also consider the benefits of a one-to-one relationship with a coach. When I ran my own business, I engaged a business coach, a woman who'd had a stellar career. Her knowledge of marketing, finance, and operations helped me address dimensions of my business where I wasn't yet proficient. Finding the right person can take time and discernment, but you will be glad you made the investment in yourself.

Whether you decide to seek out a support community or a personal coach or both, these resources will put the focus on all that you *are* accomplishing and *will* accomplish—a perfect way to drown out the fear of failure.

Fear of failure, conscious or, more often, unconscious, can also make us hesitant to take risks. Whether we are applying to or accepting a new position or launching or expanding a business, we are often reluctant to move forward. One of the reasons women have difficulty with failure is what Carol Dweck describes as a "fixed mindset." A poor outcome is seen as a criticism of your core self, rather than the effort or skills you've brought to a particular task.

I see that in clients who, when something goes wrong, are quick to believe the failure is their fault and theirs alone. I have seen it in one bad experience where a boss made a client fearful about future projects, despite her talents and great management skills.

While I can watch in disbelief as my clients do this to themselves, I can also recognize how I have done it myself in the past. For instance, in 2003, after moving to California when I had difficulty relaunching my coaching business, I quickly assumed that my enormous success in Boston had been luck and that when I moved west, my struggles were due to my being a failure at business. It took me several years to change my way of thinking to what Dweck calls a "growth mindset," where your abilities are seen as constantly evolving. Gradually, as I learned how to run my business effectively in a new context, I recognized that success came from what I *did*, rather than who I *was*.

Women's inclination to see qualities as innate, Dweck suggests, come from how we are treated early in life, at home and particularly at school. Research shows that girls are not called upon in class as much as boys, which leads to their raising their hands less often. At home, girls can be overlooked when siblings with greater needs or louder voices take center stage.

This describes my childhood perfectly. My younger sister had a physical disability, so I learned early that my role in my family was to be seen but not heard. It took me years to learn how to speak up. Recently, while completing a profile exercise, a colleague who was asked what word would *not* describe me said "unopinionated." At first I was shocked, and then I had to laugh out loud. I had finally succeeded in speaking up and being heard!

Girls receive messages that their successes are due to effort but that if they fail at something, it's because they lack ability. Boys' success tends to be credited to ability, and failure to their not applying themselves. Too often, girls are not encouraged to persevere in activities like sports, writing, music, or coding and given permission to drop out when things get difficult. But when girls give up too soon, they are robbed of the breakthrough that comes from persistence. They fail to experience that they *can do it*. Later in life, they bring to their career the assumptions they learned early on, and they are more inclined to concentrate on mastery of what they are good at than to pursue stretch experiences.

This can explain the emphasis on performance that we see in

women's careers, where they tend to do their job 150 percent while not exploring new or different positions, even when those opportunities are available. Women want to be "ready," which can be code for fear that they might fail if they venture outside their comfort zone. I have seen women stay too long in one position, rely too much on one mentor, and fail to seek or demonstrate capacity for stretch assignments—the key stepping-stones to advancement. The best antidote to the underlying fear of failure is to have others who can and will challenge you: a Lean In–style group, a business coach, a strong mentor.

We can develop resilience by paying attention to our mindset and self-concept. Bringing a hopeful attitude to what we do will help us have the courage and perseverance necessary to move forward. Starting from the inside out will help us choose goals and actions that connect to our larger vision and desires for our life. These attitudes and choices will set us up for success and protect us from the insidious fear of failure that can paralyze us. Like many of the thoughts that lead to enervating feelings that keep us from strong creative action, we can control fear of success by recognizing it as a pattern of thinking that we can choose to alter. We can adjust and reframe how we approach goals and action, so that success or failure becomes something we have achieved, not who we are. This approach will give us greater freedom from fear and greater courage to embrace risks and opportunities alike.

Internal Voices

Long before I became a coach, I grew acutely attuned to the inner conversations of women's lives—first as a nun who practiced daily prayer and meditation, and later as a developmental psychologist studying how women made sense of their experiences across a lifetime. So, when I began to work with professional women, I naturally listened intently to how my clients spoke about themselves and their lives.

Develop Internal Resilience

I learned what most women already know: that we talk to ourselves a lot and listen to our personal repertoire, which includes positive messages of affirmation, appreciation, and ambition, but also includes far more messages of guilt, criticism, and disappointment. While we might stop and recognize that we have these ongoing inner dialogues, we rarely acknowledge how negative messages receive a disproportionate amount of airtime. Rarer still is a committed attempt to practice regular recognition and praise for work well done.

One of my goals as a coach of women is to help them "catch success." By this I mean paying attention to when things go well, calling them out, celebrating them, and attaching feelings to these moments in order to make them memorable. Often when I introduce this concept in a coaching relationship, my clients are flustered and embarrassed and sometimes try to minimize. But they are always grateful. Over time, they grow to appreciate the practice, and eventually I can hear them incorporate this language into their updates. The trick is for each of us to retrain our internal dialogue so that we increase praise and reduce criticism. Doing so requires the same discipline and commitment to practice that presentation skills training does.

Retrain Your Internal Voices

Like any habit, retraining internal dialogues is a three-step process. First, you must recognize what you've been saying to yourself. You must notice if you have internal messages like *Oh, shit, I forgot to do . . .* or *I'll never make partner.* Don't try to change these verbal habits right away; rather, just observe what they sound like, what the triggers are, what the associated emotion feels like, and what follows. As with any problem to solve, awareness is the first step.

Once you begin to recognize the triggers, emotions, and verbal patterns, you can begin to move your awareness to the actual moment when you engage in self-talk. Start to hear and feel yourself say negative things: "I'll never get this done"; "There I go again, letting him talk and drown me out." Become aware of what it feels like to hear yourself speak this way. Before you can change this kind of habit, you need to feel it coming on. You need to move your awareness up to the nanosecond before you act.

Finally, when you're very conscious of the patterns, you can begin the effort to stop. This is where the change becomes actionable. Why is this so important? We are increasingly aware of the impact of our thinking on our health. Doctors advocate meditation as a way to reduce stress. Courses on mindfulness have swept through universities like Yale and tech companies like Google. While many of these approaches advocate stillness and silencing our inner dialogues, we also need to manage the messages that dominate our workdays.

The good news is that we have the power to manage and change these inner dialogues. The best place to start is wherever we already engage in positive messages. We know that amplifying the positive is more powerful than trying to erase the negative. One of my favorite stories from childhood is about a bet that the sun made with the wind. The sun bet that she could get a man on the street to remove his jacket faster than the wind could. The wind took the bet and began to huff and puff and blow and blow. The man pulled his coat more tightly around him with each wave of cold air. When the wind knew he was defeated, it was the sun's turn. She beamed at the young man, sending wave upon wave of warmth his way. As he relaxed into the warm air, he eventually became so hot that he removed his jacket. I tell this story often because I believe it is rich in wisdom about how to treat others *and* ourselves.

I have developed a practice of self-affirmation where I cheer myself on with the phrase "You go, girl!" when I have done something well—especially something challenging. I bring this same attention to my clients. I try to "catch success" and cheer them on as they develop new habits, engage in new behaviors, take new risks. We all need to celebrate successes, no matter how large or small. It keeps joy in our hearts and confidence in our spirits.

Another approach to ground yourself is to develop and use a favorite mantra. I had a colleague who carried a card in her wallet that said, "Courage is fear that has said its prayers." It was a constant reminder of her capacity for courage. Michelle Obama introduced the world to her response: "When they go low, we go high," which could easily become a mantra to remind yourself to be less reactive, or to combat negativity with positivity. My favorite mantras for my clients are "Have confidence in your competence" and "Keep your eyes on the business." Choosing a phrase or message as your personal mantra (the shorter the better) and writing it down someplace where it will be visible to you can reinforce an important message that you want to remember. It is another way of using the silent but resounding conversations we have with ourselves for our own benefit.

Silence the Negative Voices

Of course, some inner voices are not helpful. We need to recognize these bothersome voices so they can eventually be silenced, or at least managed. Two voices women typically hear a lot are those that lay guilt on us and those that make us feel like a fraud. Their sources and triggers may vary, but they both minimize the value and contributions we bring to others and to an organization. They are the opposite of the positive self-messages I described above. And they can have an iron grip on a woman and make it harder for her to grow in confidence and courage and have the successes she desires and deserves.

My favorite definition of guilt is an unhappy feeling that you have because you have done something wrong or think you have done something wrong. In my experience, women feel guilty far more often about things they think they *haven't* done than about any actual wrongdoing. Our expectations of ourselves are often astronomically high, beyond even the capacities of a superhero. An incessant clock and calendar remind us of meetings, projects, to-do lists, parties, emails, family, colleagues, bosses, direct reports, etc. We run like the proverbial hamster on a wheel, trying to keep up with overprogrammed weeks, days, and hours. These noises can deafen us to the sense of calm and inner conviction that enables us to know what we really want and to have the authority to pursue those desires.

We need to let go of the voices that push us to constantly attend to others, rather than ourselves. We need to actively work to stop inflicting guilt by examining the voice that we hear. We should treat the world "guilty" as an obscene expression in our heads. We can change that habit if we try.

I know that to pay attention to ourselves is easier said than done. You don't win the battle with guilt by saying, "I won't feel guilty." But an emphasis on positive self-messages, as I discussed earlier, *does* work. It's sort of like the instructions on an airplane to put on your own safety mask first before helping someone else. We can change our feelings of guilt by transforming our inner dialogue. A wise psychologist once told me that guilt is the only emotion we inflict on ourselves. If this is so, then it's in our control to change its power over us.

Another insidious voice that makes us feel fraudulent has a name: impostor syndrome. This phenomenon was originally identified by Peggy McIntosh at Wellesley College in a classic 1992 paper, "Feeling Like a Fraud." She describes how a woman can experience a set of feelings that causes her to doubt her accomplishments and continually fear that she will be exposed as a fraud and her success will crumble.

I encounter impostor syndrome often. One client, Jessica, had a big success at work. When I congratulated and praised her, she launched into all the things she could have, should have, would have done better if she had had more time. She told me how relieved she was that her boss had not been at the presentation and hadn't seen the mistakes she made.

Another client, Nora, was selected to run the major launch of a new product. Her fear that she was not competent enough, that she would fail, and that her career would be over were distressing to me, given what I knew about her track record and the enormous respect others had for her. And yet I related too, because I feel it myself when I'm with a group of highly talented women and ask myself, *What am I doing here?*

One solution to dealing with impostor syndrome is to reframe your picture. When I wonder if I belong, I recall what I have accomplished and what my friends and family think of me, and I try to relax. Then I consciously turn my focus away from myself and toward the business at hand. When I look at the job to be done, the connections to be made, or the other people I can empower, I forget about my fear of being "found out as a fraud." Returning my focus and vision to the business once again is a great source of grounding and confidence.

Guilt and impostor syndrome are forms of self-criticism. The language we use in thinking about ourselves, our actions, and how we belong can lead to feelings of incompetence. Or we can change the language we use, the stories we remember, the feelings we obsess about to build our inner self-support.

Once again, the use of language in relationship to ourselves is totally within our power. It is incumbent upon us to become virtuosos of self-praise and self-encouragement. If we can achieve confidence in our competence, we will have a much easier time focusing on the business at hand, and that in turn will lead to greater success. Michelle Obama, in her memoir, *Becoming*, speaks about how journaling helped her to track and process what was happening in her life. Journals can be used to record events, feelings, or how you are making progress toward changing a habit. The process of writing can be a dialogue with yourself, where you can see what you are thinking and feeling. Putting thoughts and feelings into words is a powerful way to name and claim them. But remember to use your journal as a vehicle to build your strength and your resilience.

It is critical to keep in mind that resilience is not achieved on your own. It requires a personal team, which can include a coach, a mentor, friends, colleagues, and family. This team will provide insight, support, feedback, cheerleading, and even a nudge, when necessary, as you grow into the successful leader and woman in authority whom you aspire to become. You must think of yourself as the general manager, finding, engaging, and mobilizing these supporters. You must craft your master plan for how they will enable you to build your resilience and how they will be there to help you sustain and maintain it over the long haul.

You may wonder why I have spent so much time addressing resilience in a book about leadership and authority. It's simple: Women need to learn early and often how to build the resilience to keep going, to develop a thick skin against negative comments. As Ruth Bader Ginsburg once said, "When a thoughtless or unkind word is spoken, best tune out." Resilience and perseverance are essential, and they are within *your* power to develop.

Today we have images of resilient women all around us, in government, business, health care, education. These women are both leaders and frontline providers. It is up to each one of us to move beyond feeling inspired and to begin to make their mindset, their sense of hope, our own. We need to retrain our inner voices to build a more resilient inner dialogue for the work that lies ahead, so that we too will be the resilient leaders the world so desperately needs.

Chapter 2: Develop Internal Resilience

Summary

- Women do an excellent job of developing their competence but fail to bring the same time and energy to building their self-confidence.
- Confidence can accrue from expertise and experience but doesn't necessarily transfer to the internal dimensions of self-image, mindset, and attitude.
- While confidence ranks among the key leadership proficiencies, women struggle to *internalize* and manifest this essential attitude.
- The greatest impediment to women's confidence is their own negative inner dialogue: fear of failure, impostor syndrome, the perceived censure of others. You must learn to manage the volume of these voices, even if you can't turn them off.
- A key antidote to the negative inner critic is amplified affirmative voices. Recall successes of the day; visualize and remember how you *felt* when things went well. Build new muscle memory in the internal vocal space. Do that for other women.

Do the Work

Learn:

- Describe in your journal the competencies that you know you possess.
- Identify the settings and situations where you feel confident about these strengths.
- What inner dialogue could you initiate to celebrate and reinforce these accomplishments? Consider writing about them in your journal to savor these moments

55

and better own your competencies. Find someone you can share these with: a friend, a colleague, or, even better, a boss.

- Consider what circumstances can lead to doubt or questions about your leadership abilities. How do they make you feel? Do they trigger memories of previous experiences?
- Pay attention to the negative internal voices when they appear. How do they make you feel? Write about it in your journal. Try to reframe this voice, or develop a new voice that allows you to be more compassionate toward yourself.

Engage:

- Identify someone to provide a corrective perspective on your inner critic: a friend or colleague, mentor or coach, therapist or counselor.
- Determine how they can help you manage your inner critic dialogues.
- What positive messages about your leadership do you want them to reinforce?

Articulate:

- Identify which inner-critic voice you will focus on first. Be specific.
- Commit to a time each week when you will write about your experiences with this voice.
- Where possible, share your process with a friend as accountability buddies.

Do It:

- Pay attention when your inner-critic voice appears, and process it in writing after the fact.
- Recognize and name the feelings that accompany this message. Just observe the feelings and the dialogue.

Develop Internal Resilience

- Over time, as you become more attentive in the moment, and begin to sense the feeling/voice emerging, notice that you will be able to shut it down.
- Amplify your moments of success.
  - ▸ Play it over in your mind (the way you might with something that goes wrong).
  - ▸ Share it with a friend or family member who delights in your success.
  - ▸ Write about it in your journal.
  - ▸ Incorporate it into your answer when asked, "What's new?"

CHAPTER 3

Women in Authority over Other Women

Women have lived and worked with other women since the time of hunters and gatherers. But more often than not, they have historically worked *for* men. They have been subservient in the workplace and at home—as secretaries to executives, nurses to doctors, teachers to male principals, wives to husbands. While women make up half the population, they have rarely been the ones in roles of authority.

In government, women comprise only 24 percent of the Senate and 27 percent of the House of Representatives. Nationally, they are mayors in only 23 percent of large cities. In business, only 7.4 percent of Fortune 500 CEOs are women; one, Roz Brewer, a Black woman, was tapped to be Walgreens' CEO in early February 2021. Only 22.5 percent of board members of Fortune 500 companies are women, and only 4.6 percent are women of color.

At the same time, the number of women-owned businesses grows at an amazing rate. In 2017, there were more than 11.6 million women-owned businesses in the United States, employing nearly 9 million people and generating $1.7 trillion in sales that year. Almost half (5.4 million) of these are majority-owned by women of color, employing 2.1 million people and generating $361 billion in revenue. Yet studies of women in authority roles are few, and little attention has been paid to women in such roles in general.

Until recently, the literature on women in authority has also been quite sparse. Yes, there are memoirs by women who have achieved success, but they are retrospective stories by superstars, such as *Own It*, by Sallie Krawcheck, and *Becoming*, by Michelle Obama. One major exception is *Lean In*, by Sheryl Sandberg, which addresses the major hurdles, both personal and systemic, that keep women from advancing to leadership positions in the workforce. Sandberg addresses how discrimination and family-unfriendly policies have played major roles in impeding women's advancement, pushing them to "lean in" at work and at home to get what they need for their careers. The book has been criticized for putting too much responsibility on the individual woman, rather than on the underlying structures, and seems targeted to high-achieving women of privilege. Nonetheless, it jump-started conversations at every level of business, was a catalyst behind many corporate initiatives, and launched Lean In Circles, which have provided support to women around the world.

Another book that has made a key contribution is *How Women Rise*, by leadership experts Sally Helgesen and Marshall Goldsmith. Goldsmith's premise in an earlier book that "what got you here won't get you there" undergirds their argument that women need to adapt their leadership practices as they rise in organizations. The book offers much wisdom and advice drawn from Helgesen's extensive experience as an executive coach, corporate consultant, and author over many decades. Her previous six books provide a historical road map of how women have navigated the rise to roles of leadership and authority.

Women in Authority over Other Women

My experience as a Catholic nun for eighteen years piqued my interest in that relationship and afforded me a unique experience and perspective on some of the dynamics that can arise around women in power. As a young nun, I taught in a girls' private high school and lived in the community of nuns that was attached to the school. My bedroom was across the hall from the headmistress's bedroom. During the day, as the school principal, she had authority over me, a member of the faculty. But after-hours, we were equal members of a community where a different woman served as community coordinator. Many times, these different roles and relationships became quite uncomfortable. I found it difficult to switch gears and figure out how to relate to her at different times of day.

As a nun, I also learned that different women hold the power and authority that come with their leadership roles in dramatically different ways. My order of nuns was international, with a leadership team drawn from countries as diverse as Spain, Ireland, India, Uganda, and Argentina. I watched how age, personality, country, and family of origin all contributed to how the women around me held and exercised authority. At the same time, I witnessed how these women overcame differences to live the motto of the order: *Cor unum et anima mea*—one heart and one spirit. All of this informed my doctoral research, in which I studied the psychological dimensions of holding authority for women, and in particular what it is like to have authority over other women. Was the experience of women in all-female environments, such as the convent, women-led startups, women-owned businesses, or non-profit organizations, different from that of women in male-led corporate environments?

Before I present what my research on women in authority revealed, I want to step back and take you on a brief journey into how I conducted that research. The approach was relatively new, remarkable in its simplicity, and startling in how readily it revealed core psychological truths. If you're tempted to skip over a discussion of the research, let me assure you that this will not be about statistical significance or comparisons to a control group. Rather, it will give you a glimpse into a new approach, developed by a team of women psychologists at Harvard who carved out a way to listen to girls and women without starting from a male norm.

LISTENING TO WOMEN

As I explained in the introduction of this book, I went to Harvard to study women's psychology with Carol Gilligan because she had developed a research methodology that focused on listening to the voices of women and girls. Her 1982 book, *In a Different Voice*, through its examination of interviews with girls and women, uncovered an alternative story of human experience, a different story of relationships, and thereby expanded our understanding of developmental psychology.

I read her book in 1984 while engaged as a career counselor for young women who were planning to become nuns, and it helped me understand the stories I was hearing from the women I interviewed in a way that the existing body of vocational literature had failed to do. Gilligan's framework explained what I was encountering in the women's stories—an ethic of care that drove them to want to live a life of service. I decided to go to Harvard to study with Gilligan so that I could reframe vocational counseling for nuns, in light of her work.

Once I was at Harvard, I learned that Gilligan had turned her attention to how this "different voice" had evolved developmentally in women. To that end, she had set out to study young girls ages nine to sixteen.

Gilligan and her team of researchers started by creating a protocol that included many open-ended questions that would give the girls in their study a greater opportunity to speak about their own experiences. The researchers also wanted to pay attention to how the girls spoke, believing that even the hesitations and the interjections the girls used had meaning. The interviews were transcribed verbatim, including "ums," "uhs," and pauses. The researchers also tracked the noticeable nonverbal signals the girls provided as they spoke about issues and challenges they faced in their lives.

When the tapes were transcribed, a team of researchers worked together to read each girl's transcript twice, each with a different purpose. The first time through, they wanted to identify the story or plot—namely, what relationship story was the girl telling? Who were the players? What was the role of the girl in the story?

The second reading resembled a biblical exegesis, where the researchers examined the language closely for patterns, meaning, and choice of words. Were the pronouns used in the subjective or objective case? Did the girl describe herself as the one in control, as an actor, or did she convey that she was acted upon? By the end, the researchers had identified what relationship story the girl had told and what role she herself played in that story. Over time, the research also uncovered particular word patterns that appeared repeatedly in individual interviews.

First, the expression "you know" occurred at moments when a girl seemed to feel safe and to trust the interviewer. Eye contact would often be made as she used "you know" to signal that she wanted the interviewer to stay connected, to understand, to join her in the knowledge she was sharing. Rather than being an extraneous phrase that could be ignored or not heard (or omitted in a text transcription), this expression was a signal to the interviewer that what followed was something true, something that mattered. Reading the interviews with this new awareness, the researchers identified the phrase as a lens that uncovered insights into the concerns and beliefs of these young women.

The second verbal cue, "I don't know," signaled a totally different dynamic. Instead of confirming safety about what she was saying, this phrase appeared when a young girl was speaking about something that felt too risky or frightening to verbalize. It signaled that the connection between the girl and herself, as well as the girl and the interviewer, was tenuous at best. These moments seemed to point to a process of dissociation in which the girls were disconnecting from their thoughts, feelings, or sense of identity.

Observing this psychological dynamic play out, the interviewers were curious to see firsthand how girls lost touch with what they knew. Furthermore, as they traced this verbal cue across interviews of the same girl at different ages, they found that the use of "I don't know" increased dramatically between age nine and age sixteen.

As psychologists, the researchers were alarmed by this evidence that the girls were disconnecting from their knowledge. What had happened? Why did they no longer know what they once had known? The researchers arrived at the hypothesis that as girls entered middle school, they were much more exposed to the larger culture and its expectations, portrayals, and stories of women. These cultural norms and images had led them to lose touch with themselves.

Today, the ubiquitous presence of social media makes girls even more vulnerable to messages that can lead to dissociation. The high incidences of eating disorders, depression, and suicide that we see today testify to the challenges girls face to stay connected to themselves and develop a strong sense of self. I'm not sure that the specific phrase Gilligan's team identified—"I don't know"—continues to suggest psychological distress for girls today (perhaps the actual words have changed over time), but I imagine that if we listen carefully, we can still recognize cues, both verbal and nonverbal, that suggest when girls are at psychological risk.

UNSPOKEN EXPECTATIONS

Since my own research in 1992 was focused on women, I wanted to see if the methods Gilligan used to study girls would also uncover experiences of women in authority that had not yet appeared in the leadership or psychological literature. Did workplace culture put women at risk for dissociation the way adolescence did for girls? How did this culture, so long dominated by men, impact relationships between and among women? Would that be different in an all-female work environment? I set out to find answers by interviewing a diverse sample of women who had all held authority roles in relationship to other women.

Using an approach similar to the one Gilligan took with the girls she studied, I conducted interviews with women and examined the transcripts for evidence of the verbal cues "you know" and "I don't know."

The first interview to offer new insights was with a woman named Sharon. When I called to arrange our meeting in the lobby of the Harvard Kennedy School building, she laughed and said, "I'm Black and six foot two—you can't miss me." A week later, on a raw November day, she arrived in an elegant, calf-length fur coat and high leather boots—a marked contrast with the down jackets and hiking boots that were de rigueur in Cambridge. She was right: I recognized her immediately. We headed to the office I had reserved for our interview.

At once relaxed and energetic, Sharon told me that she was a state councilwoman from Texas and commuted three days a week to attend the master's in public policy program at Harvard. She expressed how her husband was providing additional support for their children at home, given her current schedule. She demonstrated confidence and warmth and exuded ease. So when she began to fidget and pull at her boots in the middle of the interview, I made a quick note to examine that part of the interview once it was transcribed. *What led to this kind of nonverbal behavior?* I wondered.

Two weeks later, the transcripts arrived, and after a quick initial read, I couldn't resist going to the section of the story where

Lead

Sharon had begun to act differently. As I read the transcript aloud, I could picture the two of us in the office. She had told me about an instance when she had brought a piece of legislation to the floor of the state congress and had encountered resistance from two other council*women.*

"If it was with a man, I mean, I just expect that, *you know*, I'm going to get this straightened out. I'd go up to major chairmen of a major committee and say, 'Let my damn bill out. . . .' I have absolutely no problems with that, but with a woman, *I don't know . . . I don't know.*"

She paused and continued, "*I don't know* . . . I could very easily have gone up to the women and done the same thing . . . *I don't know.* Really, *I don't know*, I never really thought about it until right now. And, as I said, I'm very comfortable in confronting men; I don't lose a night's sleep . . ."

As I read along, I was transported back to our meeting. I could see again how she had looked away, paused, and then looked me right in the eye. Her voice had become softer and higher in pitch as she continued, "Whereas if that happens to me with a woman, I think about it a long time, and, I mean, I don't take it home with me, but then sometimes I do, and, *I don't know*, I guess there's an expectation that women, I guess, are supposed to be more sisterly and help each other and be there for each other, and then when that doesn't pan out, then I guess there's a sense of a void; something's not right, and [I ask myself,] *What did I do wrong? . . . I don't know.*"

As I reread the excerpt again, I suddenly saw that Sharon had used the phrase "I don't know" nine times in two hundred words. Here was the key verbal cue that had appeared in Gilligan's research with adolescent girls. I read and reread Sharon's words. One line in particular tugged at me on a visceral level.

"I guess there's an expectation that women, I guess, are supposed to be more sisterly and help each other and be there for each other, and then when that doesn't pan out, then I guess there's a sense of a void; something's not right, and [I ask myself,] *What did I do wrong?*"

As I studied this one long sentence, I could see that there were two statements embedded in it. First, Sharon identified her expectations of how women should be toward each other: "Women, I guess, are supposed to be more sisterly and help each other and be there for each other." Her second assertion, "When that doesn't pan out ... something's not right, and [I ask myself,] *What did I do wrong?*" acknowledged that when expectations were not met, she put the blame on herself. When something was "not right," she asked herself, *What did I do wrong?* rather than considering that the other person involved might have some responsibility for the way things went.

Sharon had told me that with men she was able to address conflict and disappointment externally but that she didn't confront the offender when that person was a woman. Instead, she suffered an internal feeling of emptiness and the sense that something was off kilter. Unmet expectations led to self-blame.

With both her verbal and nonverbal cues, Sharon led me to see a potential psychological dimension of authority for women: Women have unspoken, and even unacknowledged, expectations of other women that appear rooted in identity, rather than role, and when those expectations are not met, self-doubt and self-criticism follow.

In my academic research and later in my decades of coaching women leaders, I have learned that women, like adolescent girls, provide the verbal cues for others to understand what is going on inside them. Sometimes they actually use the phrases "you know" or "I don't know." Other times, they reveal the truth through a phrase of their own, their tone of voice, a report on an inner dialogue, or a conversation that suddenly has the sound of a siren screaming, *Listen to me! Hear this*! While they also engage in nonverbal gestures and movements, like Sharon's pulling on her boots, I have come to trust the verbal cues. In fact, I have found that quite often during a coaching session conducted over the phone, my audial antennae are even more attuned because no visual distraction is happening. I continue to hear women speak about their expectations of other women and their fears of what other women might want from them.

This dynamic may be generational, and young women today may in fact have figured out how to work together with other women in a more collaborative and connected fashion. But the systems within which we all live and work are much slower to change. Furthermore, our world of work has five generations present, which means that we do well to remember that our experiences and our journeys have been quite different. There is both wisdom and new perspective to be shared if we can find the courage to check things out when confusion, difference, or a sense of unspoken expectations or assumptions occurs.

There are three concrete steps we can each take to forge relationships with other women and overcome any challenges that threaten to break our bonds. The first is to reach out and build the relationship early on, before anything negative can happen. I am always urging my clients to connect with their female peers—to understand their part of the business and their challenges, to know how they can help. This is particularly true at more senior levels or whenever you are one of the few women at your level. You need to know that your experience is not unique. But it is also true that when you know your female colleagues better, you will understand when their choices are different than yours. A shared gender identity doesn't mean you will agree on all things. The better you know each other, the more space and freedom this differentiation will have.

The second step is a discipline that applies across all relationships: When in doubt, check it out. You will find that taking the initiative to check something out is one of the surest ways to strengthen a relationship. It is also a discipline that can become a natural practice with sufficient repetition. If you do it often enough with enough people, you will begin to do it instinctively.

The third is to build alliances, not just relationships, across the business with other women. Most of us are inclined to turn to our friends and others who share our beliefs and experience, people with whom we are comfortable. The greatest opportunity to effect change is when we turn to those who are different from us in identity, role, position, or personality and become allies. Together we can accomplish what neither could alone. As women, we have the opportunity to reach out across our differences on specific issues. We have the chance to figure out how to work together, how to truly collaborate, and how to demonstrate to others what that looks like and how it works.

SPLIT VISION

Using this method of listening to key verbal cues opened up a second fundamental psychological dynamic: split vision. While a great deal has been written about how to balance work and family, I believe other tensions and splits in women's lives are equally worrisome but often go undetected.

Take Rachel, for example. A petite woman with frizzy black hair and bright, dark eyes that framed a large sharp nose, she was a midlevel manager at a nonprofit, where her direct reports were all women.

When we met, her tiny hand shot out from the sleeve of her North Face parka. "Hi, I'm Rachel. You must be Ellen."

Her handshake was firm, consistent with the confidence she conveyed in her greeting. As she removed her woolen scarf and bulky down coat, she joked about life in the frigid Northeast. While it was not new to her, she admitted she often wondered why she hadn't gone to Stanford, where the weather was wonderful.

Rachel told me about the women she worked with. "We get along, and most of the time we work well together as a team," she said. "But sometimes it falls to me, as the person in charge, to make decisions, and that's hard." When I asked her about her experience as the woman in authority, her cadence slowed; she spoke deliberately and reflected in real time on being the boss of her all-female team.

"I was hoping . . . always trying to make the decisions that were right . . . but also hoping that it wouldn't have negative consequences on the relationships."

Pausing, Rachel fiddled with the ring on her right hand before looking up. Staring directly at me, as if to ensure that we would stay connected as she spoke, she continued, "In making the decisions and executing them, I would have an eye toward sustaining and repairing and maintaining the relationship."

When the interview was over, I walked Rachel back to the entrance of the building and headed home. But my thoughts remained on our conversation. I kept returning to her comment about keeping an eye on relationships while making decisions. For some reason, that part of her interview had triggered in me an emotional reaction that was part recognition and part melancholy. What was it about her comments that had evoked such an unsettling response?

By now I had learned that my visceral reactions were internal cues of their own. I looked forward to exploring this one further once I had the transcript of our interview in hand.

A week later, when the transcript arrived, I read through the document and then returned to the section that had haunted me. I suddenly noticed that Rachel had said, "I would have *an* eye toward sustaining and repairing and maintaining the relationship." I could see in the words before me what the trigger was: She spoke of *one* eye!

I wondered: *Where is the other eye? What is its focus? What did it see? Is it something different? Are the two views simultaneous or alternating? Metaphorically, is her vision blurred or blinded when one eye is in focus and the other isn't?* I wondered if the physical experience of eyes gazing in different directions could offer insight into the experience of split vision that Rachel had described.

I called a friend who had had this condition when she was young. "What was it like when you had a 'lazy eye' while you were growing up?" I asked. "Could you see out of both eyes or just one at a time? Did it make you feel dizzy?"

She replied, "I remember my mother taking me to the doctor, and he told us I would go blind in one eye if we did not correct the condition. He gave me exercises to do every day. I hated doing them, but eventually my eyes focused in the same direction."

"Why did he say you would go blind if you didn't do the exercises?" I asked.

"Because the brain couldn't sustain the competing input coming from two eyes looking in different directions. Eventually the brain would shut down one of the eyes."

As she recounted the doctor's counsel, I began to wonder if there was a parallel for women in authority. Did Rachel's description of keeping "*an* eye on the relationships" point to an experience of split vision that was similar to a lazy eye? I knew that women like Rachel who kept their focus on the relationships at work were often told they were too "soft" and would not make good leaders. I had also witnessed the opposite—where women who acted assertively were branded as "aggressive," as "pushy," or as a "bitch boss." I could imagine how split vision could be a useful metaphor for how women experience holding a role of authority.

Most women aren't surprised to hear about this kind of psychological split in the account of a woman who has authority over other women. In fact, keeping one eye on the relationships and one eye on roles and responsibilities is part and parcel of life for many of us. We experience the considerable pull that occurs when we try to draw two fields of sight into a single vision. This metaphor of *split* vision captures the struggle women in authority grapple with all the time—they must keep their sight clear and focused when they are pulled in two or more directions. The image presents a sort of double bind, in which women are expected to be both warm and nice and at the same competent and strong.

I wish an analogous form of vision training existed, one that would enable women to align their split vision into a single vision—but, unfortunately, no such simple solution is available. As with eye treatments, each of us must diagnose the exercises and practices that will build on our strengths and bring this creative tension into focus. One approach that can be useful is drawing attention to the future—the direction you are pursuing, where you are moving your organization, what lies ahead. This can help you move beyond an either/or paradigm of balancing like a seesaw between relationships and responsibilities and instead direct your energies toward a combined effort to attend to people and business. By keeping your sights on the future—your eyes on the prize, so to speak—you are steering yourself to integrate responsibilities and relationships. Using the future as your point of reference enables you to think about your responsibilities not only to the business but to the people involved.

INTERSECTIONALITY

Beyond the challenges of unspoken expectations and split vision that we may experience at the individual level, women also encounter important challenges and opportunities that accompany the diversity between and among women in the workplace. Differences in identity characteristics—race, class, sexual orientation, generation/age, parental and marital status—have always been present, but our collective awareness and willingness to acknowledge this diversity have only recently begun to gain serious recognition and understanding.

In the past, most, if not all, of us have seen and acknowledged the tension that can occur between women who are mothers and those who are not. Assumptions about commitment and availability can be made by women about each other, based on whether or not they have children. But there is no question that a much bigger challenge is how racial identity impacts women's career trajectory.

Historically, this issue has been overlooked far too often. In the wake of the Black Lives Matter movement, however, a new urgency regarding racial justice has brought attention to the experiences of women of color, who encounter both racism and sexism not just at work but in society at large.

Since the Black Lives Matter movement began, white America has begun to realize how our privilege has kept us from knowing and understanding the history and reality of racism in the United States and in particular the world of business. Many of us are now seeking to educate ourselves and have been helped by excellent books like *Caste* (Isabel Wilkerson), *Biased* (Jennifer Eberhardt), and *How to Be an Antiracist* (Ibram X. Kendi). Each one opens a door on the history behind the systems that have brought us to this moment. Other books, like *White Fragility* (Robin DiAngelo), have drawn heat for being geared toward white readers, since their focus tends to be on making the topic comfortable and palatable for that audience. While this may be a "soft" entry into a painful subject, it runs the risk of failing to grasp the true systemic, relational, and individual hostilities, discrimination, and inequalities that women of color have experienced. The goal cannot be about becoming "woke" as white people. The goal must be about gaining equity and justice for all—especially those who have not been treated equitably because of the color of their skin. We have a long way to go to fully appreciate the challenges women of color have faced in traditionally white organizations, and much work to do.

Black feminist scholar Kimberlé Crenshaw coined the term "intersectionality" in 1989 as the study of where different aspects of our social identity overlap or intersect. This lens helps us to address and begin to understand how women of color experience both racism and sexism in the workplace. They experience racism differently from their Black male colleagues, and they experience sexism differently from their white female colleagues. The double impact of their vulnerability not only is twice as difficult but can be twice as isolating. We have heard this story frequently in the discourse triggered by the deaths of George Floyd, Breonna Taylor, and countless other Black victims of police violence.

Intersectionality is an important lens to bring to how we think about women in authority over other women, especially when a woman who enjoys white privilege is in a position of power and authority over a woman of color, or the other way around. On some level, the woman of color will be more acutely aware of the residue of generations of inequitable racial relationships than white women are. The awareness may be unconscious, it may be unspoken, but it will most likely be felt by one group and not necessarily by the other.

In 2020, I attended a webinar with a group of highly accomplished women who were talking about a worldwide conference they had attended. One commented on a presentation by Isabel Wilkerson, the Pulitzer Prize–winning, Black author of *Caste*, and mentioned being struck by how "articulate" she was. I was immediately taken aback at the comment. I was aware that this word has a history of being used in reference to Black women and men, as if to say, "How surprising that they can speak so well!" It is certainly not a word that we would use to describe a Pulitzer Prize–winning white author.

I looked around the Zoom screen to see how other participants were reacting and tried to catch the eye of a Black colleague of mine, Ruth, but could not. As my mind raced, trying to process what to do, I heard my inner excuses—*You were not there; this is not a discussion, it is a report; this person did not ask for comments or questions*—and I remained silent.

Women in Authority over Other Women

Ruth and I belong to an organization of professional women and have been working alongside several other women to identify how we can address issues of racial equality individually and collectively. The following week, we were discussing the topic of microaggressions, and Ruth brought up our experience on the call. When she finished sharing her perspective, I jumped in and shared my experience of being silent, and my realization—a bit late in coming—that this kind of silence is no longer acceptable.

Our group's ensuing discussions regarding the word "articulate" led to several insights for all of us. The two Black women in the group educated the rest of us about the extent to which language has different meanings for different people. Others spoke of how they loved the word and meant no harm by using it. We also agreed that intention doesn't dismiss impact. Saying, "I didn't mean to offend" does not make what someone said less offensive.

I came away from this conversation with a renewed conviction that each one of us is responsible for continuing to educate ourselves about white privilege and antiracist practices in order to speak with awareness and take informed action as leaders in our own organizations and communities. Working together in this group has given all of us the experience of building bonds across differences and seeing how we can work as allies within a group.

Over the past few years, I have come to recognize that in my own work on behalf of women, I have shown my own blindness and silence. Despite my passion for working on behalf of all women, I failed to see that my clients were mostly white women—in fact, mostly white and heterosexual women. I failed to see how often no women (or men) of color sat at the executive table at the companies where I worked. And even when I did notice this, I failed to question my client companies about why this was the case. I failed to appreciate or address how integral a part of the work experience racism was for women of color. I say that not as an excuse but as a fact. I had opportunities to agitate for change, and I let them pass me by.

One specific incident I regret deeply today is the work I did with Linda, a Black woman I was asked to coach at a finance company in Boston. She was in her early thirties, ambitious and talented, and had a work record that would have put her on anyone's high-potential list. She was also very assertive and outspoken and worked for an Indian male executive. When their company brought me in, they already had a history of conflict over communication and "style." Today, when I look back, I see that racial differences, even issues of racism, were right there. It was the elephant in the room that no one—including me—was addressing. Although Indian by birth, Linda's boss had adopted the white social status of his colleagues in Boston. In hindsight, I suspect that the uneasiness he was feeling was due to his own discomfort with the intersection of Linda's race and gender—but the "identifying problem" was how *she* communicated.

I wish I had asked him what specific attributes he found troubling about Linda's style. Why were these attributes problematic, given her role? How had he tried to address them? Were these attributes present in other members of the team?

I still carry regret and sadness that I failed to be a true ally to Linda in that situation. I recognize today that this is how the culture of racism is reinforced and continued—because so many of us aren't attuned to its presence or courageous enough to do something about it. I hope that if I found myself in a similar circumstance today, I would speak up. I have taken the time to read and listen. I seek out opportunities to hear Black women's stories, to listen carefully, to seek honest feedback, and to partner with them to make changes. I am committed to doing the work of this journey, and to seeing more clearly.

I have learned that in some ways, white and Black women live in parallel universes, and as a white woman who has enjoyed the privilege of being part of the dominant culture, I see more clearly how I and we need to change—individually, systemically, and in relationship to each other. We need to learn. We need to listen. We need to own our responsibility. We need to train our eyes to focus not just on advancing as women but on ensuring that our female colleagues of color are advancing as well.

What is most important is where we go from here. How do we engage for the future? How do we ensure that all women have a chance to advance? How do we partner with organizations that will help us get there? Women who have learned so much about how to help each other advance are particularly poised to have the necessary conversations with our colleagues of color. Are we willing and able to do so? Are we prepared to handle the backlash we may and probably will encounter? Above all, are we willing and able to make a difference today so that the next generation of girls and women inherits a world that recognizes, respects, and engages the gifts that women—all women—have to offer?

Chapter 3:
Women in Authority over Other Women

Summary

- The relationships between women across roles of authority haven't received adequate attention in leadership literature. Yet women are holding increasing numbers of leadership positions. We must better understand the experiences of women in roles of authority in relationship to other women.
- Women in authority describe unspoken expectations that other women have of them that can make exercising their leadership more difficult.
- When there is a reporting relationship between two women of different identity characteristics, there can be additional challenges. Today as we seek to be more equitable as well as inclusive in our organizations, those of us who have enjoyed privilege as white women have a lot to learn and a lot of work to do to support women of color within our companies and communities.

Do the Work

Learn:

- Write in your journal about unspoken expectations you have held of other women in roles of authority. What were the circumstances? Were you able to speak about them? What did you learn? How do they inform your work today?
- Have you experienced unspoken expectations from another woman when you were in a role of authority? What was that like? How did the expectations impact

your working relationship? Were you able to address them? What did you learn?

- Have you been in a role of authority where women reporting to you were a different race, sexual orientation, or parental status?
- If you are a woman of color, how have unspoken expectations impacted your career? What do you expect from your relationships with your white female colleagues? What do you experience within these relationships?
- If you are a white woman, have you been aware of how white privilege may have helped your career? Have you seen or taken opportunities to be an ally to women of color in the workplace? Have the activities following the Black Lives Matter movement brought new insights? What are they, and what can you do as a result?

Engage:
- Find a colleague who is not necessarily a friend. Discuss your experiences of expectations and intersectionality across roles of authority at work.
- Organize a group of women to consider issues of authority for women. How have differences in identity characteristics impacted your relationships with other women in authority roles?
- If you are a white woman, is there a person of color in your organization to whom you could reach out? Begin by asking if she is willing to have a conversation about what her experience has been. If she is willing, when you have this talk, be honest about your own journey. Try to name any blind spots that you realize you have had in the past. What are you doing about them now? How could you be a better ally?

Lead

Articulate:
- Initiate or get involved in your company's diversity, equity, and inclusion initiatives.
- Pay attention to microaggressions in meetings; speak out when women of color are silenced or overlooked.
- Do your homework and be prepared to discuss racial or gender injustice intelligently.
- Cultivate male allies and be prepared to have intelligent conversations with them about what they can do to support you and other women.

Do It:
- I will examine my unspoken expectations by _____.
- I will examine unconscious bias in my own organization and personal behavior by _____.
- I will become an ally for women of color in my organization by _____.
- I will continue to educate myself by _____.
- I will forge relationships with other women at my level in my organization by _____.

CHAPTER 4

———

Executive Presence

A new engagement for me to coach a high-potential or senior-level woman has often included the directive to "increase her executive presence." In my experience, this guidance is, predictably, issued in organizations or industries with a predominantly male workforce, especially at the senior levels, and it is typically difficult to gain a clear understanding of what this phrase actually means. Over time, I have come to see that it is often used as a sort of shorthand for, "Make her a better fit with the other male executives." I understand that the company expects me to coach her on how to work with her colleagues in a way that is comfortable for them. I, however, prefer to think about the message as meaning, "Help her to effectively exercise leadership with authority."

The term "executive presence" (EP) tends to conjure up unconscious expectations of what an executive looks like and what qualities he exudes. (I say "he" because historically executives have been male—and white, and often tall.) When used to describe a man in authority, "executive presence" suggests that he is trustworthy and demonstrates the ability to exercise authority effectively. At the same time, when speaking of women in authority roles, you are far more likely to hear the term used to describe a deficit, as in "She is a high performer, *but* she *lacks* executive presence."

So, what exactly is this quality that advances men but impedes women because of its perceived absence? In her book *Executive Presence*, Sylvia Hewlett explains that EP has three components: presentation, communication, and gravitas—in other words, how you appear, communicate, and behave. But it is more than the sum of these parts. Fundamentally, EP is the impact you have on others.

Over the years, I have learned that when I am hired to increase a woman executive's EP, her employer assumes that it is a quality I can teach her to simply "put on." But for women, true EP is developed not as something added on, but rather as something from within, the outcome of becoming our truest self as a leader. As Maya Angelou reminds us, "People will forget what you said, people will forget what you did, but people will never forget how you made them feel." Developing EP is about how we make others feel. Mastering it is what will make our presence memorable.

So, how does one develop an executive presence? Let's take a look at the various factors.

MAKE A GREAT FIRST IMPRESSION

We all know that first impressions matter. When we think about our presentation, we begin with the nanosecond reaction we have when we first meet someone. As the familiar example of a limp handshake illustrates, we do judge a book by its cover, and our first experience of another person is influenced by what they look like (whether we admit it or not). Initial impressions are hardwired into humans as a mechanism to keep us safe. There was a time when we needed to be able to judge whether strangers meant us harm or good based solely on what they looked, sounded, and smelled like. Over time, we have come to judge others on elements of appearance that have little to do with safety and much more to do with preference and comfort. Grooming, hygiene, body type, fitness, clothing, makeup, jewelry, etc., all impact how we size up another person.

Just as we judge others, they judge us. Our demeanor, attitude, and nonverbal communication matter. For example, in *Executive Presence*, Mellody Hobson, president of Ariel Investments and a frequent financial commentator on CBS, tells how she learned the importance of smiling, particularly as a Black woman. This insight is similar to stories Michelle Obama has told about early perceptions of her as an angry Black woman. During her husband's presidential campaign, she was shown a video of a stump speech where the sound was turned off. She could see how her audience saw her facial expressions. What looked like passion and commitment to her could easily have been misconstrued as anger by others.

How we are perceived isn't the same as how we are feeling, but we must manage both realities. This is particularly true for women of color, who carry a much heavier burden than white women when it comes to how they show up.

Our physical appearance makes a huge difference in how we come across. The elements of dress are pretty simple and straightforward for men and much more complicated for women. For instance, men in finance know where to find the suits and ties that convey authority; their counterparts in the tech industry know that Dockers pants work unless they are engineers, in which case hoodies and slouch jeans are the uniform.

Women, on the other hand, have to be attentive to issues of cultural fit, style, color, and audience, as well as what fits their personality, role, and industry. This is a much more subtle but complex process than simply wearing clean, well-pressed clothing and shoes that do not wake the dead as you walk across a room. It involves developing a strong personal style that can project a memorable executive presence. Women can use their appearance to send a powerful message about who they are and what they value. Michelle Obama has been particularly effective at that—not only in her penchant for sleeveless dresses, but inasmuch as she has promoted otherwise unknown American stylists by wearing their clothes.

An example of how different styles can show up is evident in how the women who ran for the Democratic presidential nomination in 2020 chose to launch their campaigns. Amy Klobuchar launched her "senator from next door" campaign dressed in a down jacket in a snowstorm in Minnesota. Elizabeth Warren created a home video of herself wearing slacks and a maroon turtleneck, drinking beer with her husband in their kitchen in Cambridge, Massachusetts. Kamala Harris announced her campaign in a professional suit during an appearance on ABC's *Good Morning America* on Martin Luther King Day. Each of these moments tells us something about the candidate, providing a carefully crafted and memorable snapshot of what she wants us to know about her—who she is and how she wants to come across.

The days of a dark pantsuit "uniform" appear to be in the past. But women must be mindful that certain stereotypical clothes can send messages they might not intend. Shoes with very high heels, bangle bracelets, plunging necklines, and short skirt lengths can all send a mixed message. Style is like taste; there is a certain flavor that you like, that fits you, that is appropriate to the circumstances, and that, once well developed, can make life easier.

We have seen women successfully craft wardrobes that are dramatically different from each other. Sheryl Sandberg is known for form-fitting dresses and stiletto heels. Orit Gadiesh, chair of Bain & Company, a global consulting firm, dyed her hair purple in the 1990s. Rachel Maddow wears a black jacket every night. There is no longer one acceptable uniform for women, so the important thing to remember is that when you create your own wardrobe, you want it to signify who *you* are. What you wear is an outward sign, so you must be intentional about what you are signifying. Choose the impression you want to make.

As business makes more and more of a move toward virtual presentations from home, watch what you wear and the setting for your call. While we enjoy seeing each other's homes and laugh at video clips of pajama bottoms, why let such diversions get in the way of your message? The way you appear and configure your setting are important personal choices that can contribute to or detract from your end goal.

COMMUNICATE WITH PURPOSE

Style can help you to become memorable, but it is only one facet of how you come across. Presenting to others—whether in formal settings or in small group meetings—is a major part of every leader's day and depends on far more than what you wear. Your voice, pitch, tone, volume, and body language all influence how your presentation is received. Remember that how you appear and how you present convey a message that *you* want to control.

Many adults would rather have a root canal than speak in public. I was once one of those people. Then I discovered that watching a video recording of yourself can be even worse. I had this experience when a professional videographer recorded a workshop that I taught. The cameras rolled during my talk and included the slides I presented at the front of the room. When I watched the tape several weeks later, I was initially relieved. The first few minutes were fine, not a bad start at all. But then, further along, the video came to a point where we had broken into pairs to do an exercise. The camera zeroed in on my exchange with one of the participants. As he told his story, I listened intently, my eyeballs growing bigger and bigger until the visual became frightening. Before I could post the tape on my website, I knew I had to do something about those piercing eyes. (Fortunately, I was able to edit out that section!)

I must confess that I wasn't surprised that this had happened. I had seen it before in videos and realized it was a habit that I had developed over time. When I am intent or trying to emphasize a point, my eyes pop out of my head. Many years ago, when I taught seventh-grade math, one of my students would say, "Don't look at me like that!" It was the first time I realized my eyes could be a lethal weapon. Over the years, I have learned to recognize when I am listening intently and say to myself, *Pull in your eyes!* In those moments, I try to breathe, relax, and generate connection, rather than intensity.

My desire to curb this habit comes not from vanity but from a desire not to distract. Remember, the goal of presenting is for your audience to receive the message you are trying to deliver. If your expression or body language is not intentional, it is at best a distraction and at worst a contradiction. Everything you say and do is part of how you show up, and your audience's perception of you impacts their ability to hear your message. As the communications expert Marshall McLuhan said, "The medium is the message." We are the medium that becomes the message. How we appear on camera matters!

The same is true for paying attention to how we sound. An audio recording can allow you to hear how you speak, how your delivery speed sounds to your audience, how the emotions you display come across, and how often you use embolalia—expressions like "um" and "uh." I recently listened to a webinar given by a renowned publisher whom I knew personally. We had met at a conference and had hit it off. I thought she was brilliant and funny and had looked forward to the session. I was stunned to hear the "ums" and "uhs" and other hesitant language she used as she spoke. Was this the same person as my acquaintance? I wondered what it was like for those who had no other context to assess her competence.

I have learned over the years that very often people are not aware of what they are doing that impedes their success. So, after the webinar, I decided to call and offer the publisher my feedback.

She was happy to hear from me but discouraged by my feedback on her "ums" and "uhs." No one had ever mentioned this habit to her before. She thanked me and said she would review the tape of her talk to better understand what I was saying. A week later, I received a lovely email thanking me for making the time and taking the risk to bring this pattern to her attention. She was embarrassed by the tape but resolved to rid herself of her distracting, hesitant language once and for all.

Recognition is the first step toward change. We owe it to ourselves to invest in the skills that will accelerate our success, and for all of us, presentation-skills training is a key area of investment and a necessary tool for successful communication. For women, it is essential to see how you come across to an audience of one or many; doing so will help you to hone your ability to project confidence in your competence. This also includes presenting and participating on video or Zoom calls. These platforms have become an essential part of business, so we must master the virtual environment.

LEVERAGE LANGUAGE

While presentation skills are fundamental, they are ultimately only a communication tool. Your goal is to be heard, to be understood, and to be memorable. To accomplish this, your language itself must be clear, straightforward, and, above all, tailored to your audience. The good news is that what you say and how you say it is totally under your control; you can be the master of your own words. You can convey your competence in what you say by paying careful attention to both your written and your verbal language. I often tell clients to explain their message so that an intelligent eighth grader can understand it: Avoid run-on sentences; focus on the subject; employ strong, active verbs; and, wherever possible, use regular words, rather than the technical terms or jargon of your field. Most important, make every word count.

Lead

Written Communication

Karen was a VP at a global manufacturing company and had ambitions to one day be the CEO of a Fortune 500 company. She was in her late thirties, brilliant, driven to deliver results, and considered a high-potential employee. She had applied for a senior VP position that had come open at her company. One of many applicants, she had taken part in a rigorous screening process, conducted by an outside firm, which included a lengthy self-assessment and interviews with executives, her peers, and her direct reports. The feedback from the interviews was glowing: Karen was known for getting results, her people loved working for her, and she had good relationships across levels of the company. But one glaring concern emerged: Her communication was confusing and excessive.

When Karen did not get the job, she was told that this was the issue that kept her from the promotion. She committed to change her behavior and engaged me to help her make that happen.

Our initial work focused on Karen's written communication and began with a review of emails and memos she had written in the past month. I could see immediately that these messages were dense and riddled with jargon that she had acquired at a consulting firm where she had worked prior to her current position. Each sentence looked more like a paragraph. I could imagine that for a busy executive, her communications would be both time-consuming and painful to decipher.

I asked Karen to read her emails aloud. As she stumbled over voicing the complex sentences, she began to hear, as well as see, that many of the points and details she shared were unnecessary and complicated her message. This exercise also revealed another pattern I have often seen and heard in how women communicate: We walk the reader through the process that we took to arrive at an answer, rather than cutting to the chase. I don't know if this is due to insecurity or a preferred storytelling style of reporting. Either way, in a business setting, it is too much. Usually the reader—especially a male reader—just wants to know the outcome or the final decision. They don't need or expect to have to labor through how you came to it. (Be assured that if they do want that information, they will ask!)

Set the context, and get to your recommendation, proposal, or even questions as quickly and clearly as possible. Keep your messages short. Convey your point of view. Use phrases like "I propose" or "my recommendation" to demonstrate authority. Avoid the conditionals "could," "should," and "might." Try writing a draft and reviewing it with these points in mind before you send it.

Karen began to focus on what her audience *needed and wanted to know* and how that was different from what she *wanted to tell them.* She removed sentences and phrases, jargon, and unnecessary big words. A few weeks later, she told me that this exercise was forcing her to think more clearly, and in turn she found she wrote more succinctly. By reorienting her focus to her audience's needs, she developed a new way to articulate her insights and recommendations. To change her writing, she had to first change her thinking.

Avoid Tentative Language

Clear and concise language is necessary but not sufficient for a woman to be effective as a leader. Tentative language, in which a woman adds a qualifier or turns a statement into a question through an inflection in her voice, can create confusion for her audience, suggests a lack of confidence, and can rob her message of power and impact. Because it is often unconscious, this verbal tic may have a destructive impact on a woman's communication without her ever knowing why.

Deborah Tannen, in her popular nonfiction book, *You Just Don't Understand: Women and Men in Conversation*, was one of the first sociolinguists to suggest an origin for this pattern of speech. She points out how girls and boys learn from an early age a different approach to communication and language. Women and girls engage in what she calls "rapport-talk," an affiliative approach meant to foster connection, while men and boys choose "report-talk," focusing on exchanging information without paying attention to its emotional impact.

One element of the female use of rapport-talk is this use of tentative language—something that seeks to attend to the relationship while communicating. A simple example of how this difference can play out in everyday life presents itself in the way someone suggests seeing a movie. A guy is likely to say, "Hey, let's go see that new movie tonight!" whereas a woman might say, "Would you like to see that new movie?" or, worse, "What would you think about maybe seeing a movie today?" John Gray's book *Men Are from Mars, Women Are from Venus* popularized how these languages resemble speech from different planets.

Another way in which women are tentative in their language is in their use of introductory phrases, particularly when they are asking a question. For example, have you ever noticed how often women include the word "just" in a statement, as in "I was just calling to . . ." or "I just want to ask . . ."? This kind of tentative approach, so natural sounding to the female ear, may be fine in settings where rapport building is the goal. However, in workplace culture, it can inadvertently weaken the message that is being conveyed.

Another habit is to start with, "Could I ask you a question?" I once had a male colleague who, when I approached him and said, "Could I ask you a question?" would say "yes" and look away. When I stood there, he would say, "Oh, there was something else you wanted to ask me." It was his way of indicating I should just start with my question and not ask permission to ask the question. While it drove me crazy when he did that, eventually I learned the lesson: You don't need to ask permission to ask a question.

My point here is not to stress how women speak differently than men. Rather, I want to address how important it is that women make their speech clear and concise. Over time, I have found it much easier to rid my *written* communication of tentative language because I can see it and change it. As that has become habitual, I have learned how to hear these habits when I speak. Seemingly minor tweaks in our written and verbal communication at work can ultimately result in our being seen and heard.

Carol is another example of someone whose communication style almost undermined her career. She was a senior manager at a financial institution where she had been passed over for a promotion several times. Her evaluations praised her initiative, hard work, team spirit, and ability to deliver. When she asked why she had not yet been promoted, the answers were vague but centered on issues of confidence—both her own and others'. Her boss finally explained that other executives did not have confidence in her ability to assume authority over a larger organization.

When I began my work with Carol, I could see that her written work was clear and concise. She delivered reports and analyses that were well written, easy to understand, and focused on the questions at hand. However, in meetings both small and large, her language became tentative when she made a recommendation or raised a question. She repeatedly undermined her own statements with phrases such as "perhaps," "it could be," "I wonder if," and "it might be true that." This tentative language made her ideas, questions, and suggestions sound uncertain, although that was not her intention.

In addition to the tentative terms women employ, we also use other vocal cues, known as upspeak, that make us sound like we are pulling our punches. One example is a verbal tag added at the end of a sentence—for example, "She did a good job, didn't she?" This makes a statement sound like a question for which you are awaiting an affirmative response. The same thing happens when your voice lifts at the end of a sentence, making statements sound like questions, investing the hearer with the power to approve or disapprove.

Tentative language is not an innocent add-on. The inclination to speak tentatively is habitual and insidious. It is a verbal tic that strikes at the speaker's authority and weakens what she says. Eliminate it from your communication.

This is admittedly easier said than done, since doing so requires you to change how you think about yourself as a speaker and a leader and about the importance of the message you are delivering to your audience, but we can and must work at changing this habit. One simple step is to tune our ears and our eyes to hear and see it in our communication and others'. We must provide feedback similar to what a music teacher or voice coach would offer a student.

We all have a great deal at stake in gaining authority. Let's help each other get there. We can ask each other to listen for tentative language before a meeting by asking colleagues, "Will you listen for when I 'pull my punch' or sound uncertain? I'm trying to change that pattern." If you see someone undermining herself, you could point it out even without being asked. We all need help in making this unconscious habit conscious and then eliminating it.

Recognize the Power of Little Words

A discussion of language isn't complete without the recognition of the power of little words—pronouns, adverbs, and prepositions. (A quick refresher for those who need it: Pronouns are words that stand in for nouns, adverbs are words that modify a verb, and prepositions establish a relationship between words.) These words may often be small in size, but they carry disproportionate weight in the impact they have on communication.

Let's begin with pronouns. In my work with women leaders, I have found a different type of pronoun selection issue than the one most frequently talked about today—the use of "they" in the place of "he" or "she" in the singular (an important discussion, but not one we'll delve into in this book)—which is the choice between the use of "I" or "we," particularly when someone is talking about work accomplished. I have found that women are far more comfortable using the word "we" than "I" and are hesitant to claim the authority that "I" suggests.

Many argue that the plural term is more inclusive and that there is no "I" in "team." I take a different position. The collapse of "I" into "we" may be important when you are trying to communicate collaboration and shared ownership, but it can also give away power and authority. Women are too quick to share authority and not attentive enough to when they need to name and claim it for themselves.

Nancy is a good example of how the use of particular pronouns identifies challenges pertaining to authority, as well as a simple solution to the dilemma. Nancy was a senior director at an office supply company, where she was considered a high-potential employee. She was as tall as a basketball player and carried herself like a dancer. She was smart, talented, and lovely. Our initial meeting focused on a special project she had been asked to colead.

The CEO asked Nancy and her colleague Frank to investigate a new technology that could deliver an exciting customized product to their customers. They were given ninety days to research the opportunity, put together a business plan, and return with their recommendations. Every two weeks, they would report on their progress to the CEO, usually in person. It was clear to me that this project had all the elements of an important career opportunity: visibility to the CEO, starting something new, working across the company.

When we met again a few weeks later, I asked how it was going. Nancy's forehead furrowed and she bit down on her lower lip as she answered, "It's okay . . . but . . . I don't know . . . This may be silly, but . . ." After a pause, she continued, "There's this thing that happens . . . It's probably stupid . . . I'm probably just too sensitive . . . I don't know . . . but it's bugging me."

The "I don't know" was like a siren call reminding me of the research I had done at Harvard on women in roles of authority.

Since then, I had learned to listen carefully to what followed, because "I don't know" was often a verbal cue that something important was at stake behind the self-deprecating and tentative language. As we explored in chapter 3, the pattern of using this phrase was first discovered in research with adolescent girls who say "I don't know" when they touch on a topic that they fear will lead to a break in connection. In my research, I had found that the same pattern appeared when women spoke about difficult dimensions of exercising authority.

Nancy explained, "When we meet with the CEO, Frank constantly uses 'I' to report on what's been done. Over time, it's begun to sound like he's in charge, which isn't how the project was set up."

"Have you talked to Frank about this and how it makes you feel?" I asked.

Nancy shifted in her seat and explained, "No. He'll tell me I'm being too sensitive and overreacting. I will appear weak, and he's likely to take advantage of that in the next meeting."

Her story captured many familiar themes of my work with talented women: the desire to do good work and be recognized for it, an emphasis on collaboration, and a fear of confronting others. I decided to propose what seemed a simple solution to the situation. "Why not mirror his behavior and start saying 'I,' instead of 'we'?" I suggested.

Nancy's response to my suggestion was an indignant, "I could never do that." She was clearly annoyed that I suggested she use the behavior she found so offensive.

"Why not?" I asked, pushing her to explain.

"Because … because … it isn't right to say 'I' when we're coleads. *He* should say 'we.'"

"Do you know how to get *him* to change *his* behavior?" I asked.

"Well, no … That's the problem."

And that *is* the problem. Too often, we expect others to change their behavior. However, those others may not be aware of the distress that their behavior creates, and they have little to no incentive to understand or to change. Sometimes a better course of action is to change our own behavior instead—but in a proactive, not reactive, way. For Nancy, that meant making a conscious choice to name and claim her role in the project and let Frank respond to her actions, rather than continuing to react with frustration to his.

When we met a month later, Nancy's face beamed. She had begun to shift to saying "I" instead of "we," with great success. She thought that Frank was a bit miffed, but the CEO had paid attention to her remarks and responded favorably. She admitted to a new sense of authority and acknowledged her surprise at the difference this simple change in language could make.

Years later, I am still struck by the level of emotional resistance Nancy displayed when I first suggested she use the pronoun "I." The truth is that Nancy's shift from "we" to "I" was much more than a simple substitution of words; it transformed the way she viewed her authority. Initially, she wanted Frank to change, but she came to realize that she herself could alter the situation if she acted differently. Rather than continuing to back down and acquiesce, she needed to stand up in a new way, even if it was uncomfortable. Using "I" forced Nancy to step up onto the stage with Frank. She had to own her power. A different mindset and new language had a ripple effect on her communication and ultimately on her executive presence. This is a perfect example of how language not only articulates but helps to create a new reality through the choices we make in our expression and communication.

Nancy is not alone in her reticence, and even resistance, to asserting herself. I have encountered this hesitation with other clients as well. There is the seasoned VP I worked with whose expertise and business savvy are extraordinary but whose avoidance of conflict leaves her vulnerable to bullies. And the marketing executive who quickly earned the respect of her new team but was hesitant to convey a hard message to an external consultant. But with time, attention, and effort, each one of us *can* change these behaviors. We just have to make the commitment to do the work.

RECLAIM GRAVITAS

In addition to appearance and language, the third, and most elusive, dimension of executive presence is gravitas. It's a rich and robust word most often associated with men, but it's time for us to claim the term "gravitas" for women.

When I ask myself, *Who are the women who have gravitas?* a lively, energized, and exciting set of images emerges. I see women who work to make a difference in the world for others. I see two women from my past when I was a Catholic nun, women who served as Mother General (think CEO) of the Religious of the Sacred Heart. The first, Concha Comacho, was forty-two, from the Basque region of Spain, and led our order with a vibrant, charismatic energy. Her successor, Helen McLaughlin, was a Scottish woman in her sixties who had worked for years in Africa as a missionary. She was reserved where Concha was exuberant, yet they both demonstrated gravitas in the face of the powerful Vatican curia, Concha with her fiery determination and Helen with her calm deliberation.

I think of Speaker of the US House of Representatives Nancy Pelosi, who daily demonstrates gravitas on Capitol Hill, and Ursula Burns, the first Black woman to be CEO and chair of Xerox. I think of acclaimed author Toni Morrison; German chancellor Angela Merkel; media magnate and philanthropist Oprah Winfrey; Christine Lagarde, head of the European Central Bank; and, of course, Stacey Abrams, who demonstrated how to engage both new and disenfranchised voters alike in Georgia to come out and vote. But my favorite female célèbre is Greta Thunberg, the sixteen-year-old from Sweden who challenged and chastised world leaders about climate change in her talk at the World Economic Forum in Davos in 2019. In her TED talk, you can experience how her gravitas far exceeds her age. She speaks truth to power without fear or hesitation. Her awareness that climate devastation will occur in her lifetime has given her an urgency and clarity that have captivated people young and old around the world.

The question, then, is how do women acquire and demonstrate gravitas? They can do so via many different paths. The women I have worked with and observed in companies, universities, and public service have often achieved this competency through leadership roles in sports, school government, or volunteering in local organizations. Many have done so by overcoming painful personal tragedy, or through exposure to the suffering of others. Still, others have had a defining moment that sparked a passion to make a difference.

An early client of mine was the general manager of a manufacturing firm, where she led a team of men. Although she was only in her thirties, her authority and strategic vision were second nature. She attributed her gravitas to the two years she served as captain of an Ivy League women's basketball team. She had learned key leadership lessons on the basketball court: Keep one eye on the ball and the other on where you're going. Know when to pass and know when to shoot, and don't be afraid to fall down, because it's the only way to learn how to get up faster the next time.

A colleague in Silicon Valley, a woman in her fifties, had been groomed in IBM's executive training program. She had a calm demeanor that convinced all around her that she could and would handle anything that came her way. Her humor and kindness drew others to her, but her business acumen and future focus were what gave her weight.

While each of these women had her own struggles, no one questioned their gravitas. It came from the inside and showed outwardly—it was a part of how they came to work. They had confidence in their competence and knew when, where, and how to draw upon this inner strength. Their ability to be themselves across a variety of settings made their exercise of authority even more powerful.

What does all this mean for you? It means that no matter what your style or approach, it is possible to demonstrate gravitas. Winston Churchill, the stereotypical picture of male gravitas, once said, "A pessimist sees the difficulty in every opportunity; an optimist sees the opportunity in every difficulty." To paraphrase, above all, you must be an optimist about your ability to demonstrate gravitas. It begins with a mindset shift to focus on your strengths, not your weaknesses. You must be willing to let go of fears and hesitations about what you believe you are lacking. The first step toward gravitas is your belief that others will know they can trust you. Your experience and expertise are the tools you use to exercise authority, but your belief in yourself is what will allow you to achieve true gravitas.

We must also work to expand our vision of gravitas. Just as women have had to contend with male biases in terms of what executive presence looks like, there are many other ways in which unconscious biases influence our openness to job candidates or colleagues who are or appear to be different from us or what we have known. In an August 22, 2012, *Harvard Business Review* article, "Deconstructing Executive Presence," John Beeson reminds us, "In an increasingly diverse world, executive presence will look very different from one executive to another." We must welcome this diversity in how others show up, just as we expect our own unique brand of gravitas to be accepted. Citizens are voting for this diversity in their choices of candidates, and companies are implementing new policies to ensure greater inclusion and diversity in their ranks. The nomination and election of Kamala Harris as the first US vice president who is a woman of color is the most dramatic step toward recognizing and valuing this diversity.

I want to end this chapter with a personal story that was a pivotal moment for me in the writing of this book.

In November 2018, I attended the Kauai Writers Conference in Hawaii. At the time, I had completed 237 pages of a memoir, but members of the faculty saw a different book in my story and encouraged me to turn my manuscript into a leadership book about women and authority. My excitement over the new direction numbed the fearsome fact that I would need to start over.

At the end of the conference, participants were allowed to pitch their book to a panel of agents and writers. Each person had sixty seconds. I decided to go for it. I wrote and rewrote my pitch for the new version of my book. When my turn came, I began by introducing myself as Dr. Ellen Snee, though I rarely use my title. I continued, "For twenty-five years, I have been at the forefront of women's leadership development. As a Harvard academic, I studied women in roles of authority and co-led [the school's] International Women's Forum program. I founded a million-dollar consulting firm that worked with Fortune 500 companies such as Pfizer, Schwab, Marriott, and Goodyear and was later the global VP of leadership development for a Silicon Valley tech company."

The experience of claiming my authority and articulating why I was qualified to write this book was exhilarating. I felt like I had knocked it out of the ballpark. When the panel announced that I had won the contest, it was the proverbial icing on the cake and more. I had the thrill of recognition and the profound confirmation that others believed in me. I had spoken my truth and been heard, and it had made a difference.

I learned an important lesson from that experience, one that I think other women who wish to demonstrate their authority can replicate. Find a safe space to practice and to try things out. These can be ordinary meetings, a talk you offer to give, or a presentation to your boss. There is simply no better way to experience owning your truth than speaking it to others and experiencing the response and confirmation they provide. Language is pivotal to executive presence, and speaking up is a key way to express language. But remember that in order to be effective, speaking up first requires you to make an internal choice to know what you know and "go for it" by articulating what you believe.

Chapter 4: Executive Presence

Summary

- Executive presence includes how you show up and how you communicate—especially your ability to demonstrate gravitas or authority.
- How women speak is the most important dimension of their executive presence. Women who speak clearly and succinctly, with a well-modulated, deep voice, will be listened to more often. Speed, jargon, high pitch, and rambling are to be avoided.
- Women's use of tentative language, such as "I think," "perhaps," and "it might," robs their statements of strength. The habit of raising your voice at the end of a sentence, which suggests that what was said is a question and not an assertion, is also problematic.
- Asking for permission at the beginning of a sentence—"I was calling to ask if"; "I wondered if you could"; "Could I ask you to"—weaken communication. Using the hypotheticals "if," "could," "should," and "would" confuses, dilutes, and distracts.

Do the Work

Learn:

- Review prior feedback that you have received about your presence in both large and small settings.
- Study any videotapes of presentations you have given. Watch them with and without the sound, looking for verbal and nonverbal patterns.
  - ▶ Pay attention to your posture, how you make and maintain eye contact with others, and your nonverbal habits.

▸ Notice the speed you use when speaking. Do you pause? At the right places? Do you repeat unnecessary expressions, like "um" or "you know," when you are talking?

▸ Are your emotions on full display? In a way that is helpful or distracting?

Engage:

- Ask colleagues how they experience you in large and small meetings.
- Reach out to someone in your company's communications department or to an outside consultant to get an assessment of your presentation skills.
- Seek feedback on your *written* communication (emails and texts), and your verbal communication, from your boss, peers, and direct reports. Is your communication clear? Is the length appropriate? How do others feel when they see something from you in their inbox?
- Reach out to someone whose written communication you admire and respect. Ask if you could interview them about their approach.

Articulate:

- Prioritize the sequence in which you will address the dimensions of your executive presence: your interaction in meetings, presentation skills, and written communications.
- Draw on feedback you have already received to identify behaviors you want to address immediately. Write out when, where, and how you will do so. Consider engaging a colleague to provide periodic feedback if your focus is on behaviors in a group context.
- Pursue formal presentation-skills training to improve your effectiveness as a public speaker.

- Look into joining a Toastmasters International group to practice public speaking.

Do it:
- Map out actions for the year based on what is most urgent, when training is available, and what will have the greatest impact on your business. Set quarter-by-quarter objectives.
- Review the plan with your boss. Discuss opportunities for additional training and presentations. Be clear about how this will contribute to the business and increase your contributions as a leader.
- Let others know you are working on these goals and engage them in your process.

CHAPTER 5

Organizational Authority Relationships

When you work within a large organization, you need to manage in every direction. Most of us are aware of the necessity of keeping our immediate boss in the loop on what we are doing and why. Similarly, we pay careful attention to be sure we communicate with our direct reports. However, we can easily overlook the importance of staying in touch with the other executives in the organization who are in roles above us, up to and including the CEO. We can also take for granted the support systems of Finance, Human Resources, and Legal and forget to build strong relationships with them except when we have specific, urgent needs. And failure to pay attention to the power and contributions of support staff—those of our own executive assistants and of other leaders' executive assistants—happens at our own peril.

EXECUTIVES

The expression "manage up" can easily carry a negative connotation. I was told once that I was perceived as someone who liked to "manage up" because I had sent a note praising a CEO's presentation at an all-hands meeting. My purpose had been sincere, but the praise I gave to the senior executive was seen as an attempt to curry favor. I would do, and have done, it again, trusting that over time my intent would come through and my response would be appreciated. However, that negative feedback was a good reminder that communicating up with senior executives is a serious skill to develop. Executives need to know who you are, what you do, and why they should care about what you have to say. But, as with most things in life, *how* you communicate matters as much as *what* you communicate.

Several approaches can achieve success without misinterpretation. First, be consistent in your written messages to senior executives. Keep them short, to the point, and worth the time they will take to read. This could include information you have secured that the executives might not have access to—about the company, the industry, or a conversation you have had or observed on social media that covers a topic near and dear to their hearts or of serious concern to the business. Executives are human and appreciate relevant, timely information about the things that matter to them.

Second, bringing attention to a job well done by a team that is not yours gives you added credibility and enables the exec to have a third-party perspective. Or an issue that you hear bubbling up among employees and bring to the attention of the appropriate senior person can be dealt with before the matter becomes too big. An idea for a new product, service, or company activity is always a great topic for a message too.

But there are also several things to keep in mind when communicating up. Remember that if you are going over your boss's head, you are creating a difficult situation for all. Always try to bring your message to your boss first before you send it farther up the chain. And always remember that any message sent will most likely be forwarded on to others. Be sure it can withstand exposure and scrutiny.

DIRECT REPORTS

Management of direct reports is a leader's primary responsibility. Exactly how you approach this can vary according to the culture of the organization and your personality and style. But a successful relationship between a manager and her direct reports needs to address frequency and modes of communication, their understanding of delegation and accountability, and their expectations about availability. The responsibility to drive these conversations rests primarily with the manager; however, both parties should make time at the start of a new relationship to discuss how they will work together and ensure they are on the same page.

Michael Watkins, in his book *The First 90 Days*, provides a great list of questions for how to frame a conversation in a new reporting relationship. He addresses all of these key areas, noting that no one correct approach exists but that alignment and mutual understanding are musts.

Direct reports are the primary way in which you will get work done. They are also a key conduit to information and communication with the rest of your organization. You want them to know they have your trust and confidence and that you will have their back. Openness and trust will make it much easier to get at the heart of a problem, solve it together, and have a stronger relationship as you move on.

As the leader, you must also hold your direct reports accountable. For women, it is sometimes easy to slip into a friendship which makes it difficult to expect and demand that those who report to you deliver on responsibilities. The worst story I've ever heard is from decades ago, when an executive would retype letters at night, rather than address the errors with her secretary. The manager was conflict avoidant, and this seemed like a price worth paying. However, I would caution you that when the boundaries between you and your direct reports are starting to slip, ask yourself what the potential unintended consequences down the road are. Dealing with conflict doesn't get easier once a pattern of ignoring or avoiding it has begun.

EXECUTIVE ASSISTANTS

I learned early in my career that with the right assistant, I could generate results that were multiples of what I could deliver on my own. Regardless of her title, I view this relationship as a true working partnership. Beyond the usual scheduling and tracking of projects, my assistant can be a second set of eyes and ears in the organization, alerting me to concerns I may not be aware of. Of course, the danger of blurred boundaries that I mentioned above is a risk, but if you manage these adeptly and an assistant becomes your confidential advocate, as well as a super admin, you will be well served.

Let me say a word about the gender of the executive assistant (EA). I have referred here to this person as a woman because most female leaders I have seen have had female EAs. However, I have noticed over time that it is not uncommon for very strong, extroverted women to choose men for this role. I have never had a chance to ask them about this choice, and the sample size is very small, but it has always made me wonder if these women find it easier to avoid the closeness and complexity of female relationships by choosing a man for the EA role.

After two decades of work with women leaders who have accelerated their effectiveness through full utilization of support staff, I have learned some valuable lessons. For example, communication is to these working partnerships what location is to real estate: everything. I've witnessed different leaders employ vastly different styles and modes of communicating, but regular, trusted communication using all available means—text, email, phone, and in-person meetings—is key. Amanda prefers to sit down with her EA first thing every morning to review what lies ahead. Paola's assistant, Maria, works remotely, so they text and email all day long. But both these leaders determined early on the frequency and modalities of their communication, and what they could delegate or manage: schedules, travel, work with finance, oversight of projects without a consultation. When things don't work the way they hope, they reassess and adjust.

Trust on your part is critical for your EA to be able to respond to correspondence, make decisions about availability, follow up on work that is due, and have oversight of even the most sensitive information. A good example is trusting her with your calendar and only in rare circumstances going around her. And above all, when you do, be sure to let her know. How you partner with her will enable her to gain the respect and trust of others, especially the other EAs with whom she works. When their collaboration is effective, they achieve far more for everyone involved than most people will ever realize. So much of what EAs accomplish is rarely seen.

That is the point, of course: They are there to make your work and the work of your organization proceed as smoothly and effectively as possible. However, you want to be sure you find regular and appropriate ways to recognize their contributions and express your gratitude. What I have learned from watching hundreds of executives over the years is that the best expressions of gratitude are the ones that are tailored to the needs and desires of the person receiving the gift. This requires getting to know the person, understanding what will make a difference to her, and paying attention to how and when you deliver it. Sometimes that is a financial reward, sometimes recognition, and sometimes an unexpected treat. But gratitude and appreciation are essential for the countless unseen and unknown acts of care and kindness that women in these roles deliver daily.

GENERAL ADMINISTRATION RELATIONSHIPS

Since my career encompassed years as an external consultant and, later, as an internal executive, I have had the opportunity to experience and appreciate the role of other key support functions in most companies: Human Resources, Finance, and Legal—sometimes referred to as "back office" or General Administration (G&A). I will confess that in my earlier life as a consultant, my encounters with these business leaders were primarily transactional. Human Resources was often (but not always) involved in hiring me and/or my team to provide services to the company. Finance and Legal would then send contracts to sign. These documents were typically designed for firms and projects much bigger and more complex than the services we were offering—usually leadership programs for women—and so I developed a certain level of frustration with this part of the work. Yet gradually I came to appreciate the important, multifaceted role they play within companies.

One of my favorite experiences of being hired by a Fortune 500 company involved a CFO of a global tire company headquartered in the Midwest. Jocelyn, the new head of HR, was a woman who had run a line of the business, attended the Harvard leadership program that I had co-led, and proposed to the executive team that they hire Fine Line to run the new leadership development program that they were about to launch.

We gave our pitch to provide coaching to the tire company's VP women and a leadership program for fifty of their top-talent female employees. Everyone listened respectfully but without much body language. The CFO, who was male, posed a few questions and then turned to Jocelyn and asked, "Do you think this is the right thing to do?"

She said without hesitation, "Yes. I have seen and experienced Fine Line's work over the course of this year, and I am confident that what they bring to us will make a difference."

"Okay, let's do it," he said, and then stood up. "Very nice to meet you, ladies. Jocelyn will follow up with you." And he was off.

The lesson I learned that day is that the relationship you have with a company's CFO and, similarly, with its general counsel, is critical. They can be essential partners in your success, providing resources for programs and green-lighting initiatives. Never underestimate the value of a strong, trusted business relationship with the occupants of these two positions. The trust that the CFO had in Jocelyn and her judgment was tangible in that meeting and was what sealed the deal for Fine Line.

When I mentioned to Jocelyn later how impressed I was by how quickly the CFO approved the program based on her recommendation, she told me a bit more about their relationship. Prior to being VP of HR, she had been the GM of one of the business units, which had struggled to meet its targets before she took over. She had overseen a turnaround operation that led to profitable results and improvements in employee morale. Throughout this process, she had been open and transparent with Finance and had collaborated with them to ensure that they made no financial missteps in achieving successful outcomes. She had gained the respect of the CFO for her business leadership.

No matter at what level of management you are, you will have corresponding business partners from HR, Finance, and Legal. Don't wait until you need their help with a problem to get to know them. Build strong relationships with your partners. Take the initiative to seek out their advice. Listen to their perspectives and insights. They can provide vital help in avoiding costly mistakes, as well as seasoned advice on how to cut costs, manage important relationships, and understand legal limits you may need to consider. They are often tuned in to other networks of information that can be valuable to you from a business perspective. And at the most senior levels, the heads of these organizations play pivotal roles in the management and direction of the company.

As you are growing your career, make the time to learn the language of these functions. Invite them to tutor you on key HR, legal, financial, and other processes. This will improve your grasp of business concepts that relate to real work in real time. You will also earn these partners' trust and respect more quickly than if you simply abdicate responsibility to them.

The importance of these relationships, and of investing time and effort in learning from them, will serve you well now and in the future. It will give you a competitive edge.

I said in the introduction that this book doesn't cover the basics of management. It assumes that the reader has that knowledge or knows where to find it. Here, I have tried to explore some of the more subtle dimensions of relationships at work that women might not pay sufficient attention to: their peers and senior executives other than their immediate boss, and their business partners in G&A functions. If we were talking in person, I would illustrate by cupping my hands around my eyes like the blinders on a horse, and I would suggest to you that most of the time women are looking down on their work and their direct reports. They need to lift their heads, remove the blinders, look around at their peers and up at the other execs. They need to understand what *all* the leaders are doing, what they are concerned about, and how to partner with them. Managing in all directions is just that—it is moving beyond a focus on your immediate responsibilities to thinking and acting like someone responsible for the whole of the company, because that is what a leader with authority does.

Chapter 5:
Organizational Authority Relationships

Summary

- Leadership requires 360-degree vision and attention: You manage up, down, laterally, and along with other leaders.
- Women score high on the emotional quotient (EQ) competencies identified as necessary in effective leaders. They manage their direct reports well but don't always pay enough attention to relationships with peers or other executives beyond their boss.
- You can magnify your effectiveness as a leader by strategically partnering with business leaders in Human Resources, Legal, Finance, and, above all, with your executive assistant.

Do the Work

Learn to view your leadership as the captain of a team:

- Find ways to understand your peers' business priorities.
- Examine your social network within the company using a social network analysis tool. Include support staff in your organization and those in the organizations with which you interface most often.
- Seek opportunities to build relationships with senior executives in other parts of the company, especially those with whom you currently have weak links.

Engage more frequently with business partners, peers, and other executives:

- Brainstorm with your executive assistant and your business partners in HR, Legal, and Finance on how to stay current with what is happening in other parts of the business and how to build stronger ties to the leaders who are your peers.

- Reach out to your colleagues who are business leaders in international roles. Identify what challenges they face from afar and how you could become an ally if you are working at headquarters.
- Find ways to connect with your peers about what is important to them: family, sports, the arts. Keep notes that will enable you to demonstrate your interest. This generation of young fathers is happy to talk about their children. Personal connections lead to better business relationships.

Articulate:

- In your personal plan for the year, incorporate regular meetings with your EA and business partners in Finance, Legal, and HR.
- Identify three to five peer leaders across the business whom you would like to know better. Commit to quarterly communication and heightened impromptu messages, where appropriate, throughout the quarter.
- Convey to your direct reports the importance of communication and collaboration across organizations. Reward behavior that supports these goals.

Do it:

- Implement this plan for increased communication with your peers and support team members.
- Treat communication with your EA, business partners, and colleagues with the same urgency you employ for direct reports.
- Highlight contributions of business partners or team members who contribute to cross functional communication.
- At the end of each year, review your efforts and their outcome with your manager. Incorporate these goals into performance reviews of direct reports.

CHAPTER 6

―――

Career Conversations

People are at the core of any business; therefore, among a leader's most important conversations are those addressing the recruitment, assessment, development, and advancement of talent. While human resources organizations run formal programs and processes, responsibility for maximizing talent rests squarely with the leaders and managers of each team. My work with women who hold leadership roles has shown me how responsibly they embrace and execute these tasks.

At the same time, I have observed that they don't always bring the same rigor to their own career development. Reviews of how they contribute to the business (i.e., performance) and strategic discussions of what might be next for them (i.e., career conversations) are often postponed or ignored. This can lead to mistaken assumptions that delivering excellent results is all that matters to them, when that is not the case. Women move along in their careers feeling confident that the results they have produced and the responsibilities they have assumed will pay off in promotions. They are often unaware of the additional skills and experiences that are needed for senior promotions. Only strategic conversations with your boss and other senior executives will allow you to identify what you need to demonstrate to receive that much-desired advancement.

PERFORMANCE AND PROMOTION

At a major conference many years ago, I had a chance to hear Robert W. Eichinger present his extensive research on competencies associated with success in business. He addressed a particular distinction he had noticed between competencies associated with performance and those associated with promotability. These findings offer valuable insights into how we can think about performance and career conversations, and I want to take a look at those here. But before we explore Eichinger's research, let's take a moment to address where many companies are with respect to traditional performance evaluations.

In the past, performance reviews have happened in an annual cycle of appraisals conducted by the HR function, in which every employee is evaluated by her/his manager. These processes range in complexity but typically include a review of goals set a year earlier, self-evaluations, input from peers and others, in-person discussion, and final write-ups by employee and manager.

Many companies are moving away from these cumbersome processes, for many reasons. The cost in hours spent has become unsustainable, millennials expect feedback often and immediately—not a year later—and research increasingly shows how biases creep into these processes. For all these reasons, review of performance has shifted toward more frequent check-ins where the focus can be on what I like to call "real work in real time."

This requires an internal shift in how you think about a discussion of your performance. In the past, you may have felt as if it was something done *to you*, but today you should view this opportunity to ask for and gain feedback as a valuable exchange with your boss. No longer bound by the strictures of a formal process, you can now structure the conversation so that you can seek guidance, celebrate victories, acknowledge when something didn't go well, and point out things that have occurred that your boss may not be aware of. In turn, you can ask what your boss has noticed that you may not be aware of. The important thing is to develop a systematic way to get regular feedback. It is a gift that you deserve.

Eichinger's research highlights where to focus your attention during conversations with work superiors about performance. Let's take a deeper look into the findings he reported.

Performance

We'll begin by discussing people whom Eichinger identified as high on performance. They demonstrated a set of skills that together he called "getting the work out" and that were composed of five factors. People needed to demonstrate that they: had the ability to drive, were focused on the customer, had skills specific to their functional area, knew how to sequence the steps of the work correctly, and were great at keeping it all organized. These criteria did not surprise me, since most of my clients were accustomed to receiving high praise for their performance. (In fact, I have seen bosses reluctant to promote a woman on their team, for fear of losing their top performer.) However, while getting the work out was necessary for promotability, it was not the sole requirement. Eichinger cited two additional factors, each with its own set of competencies, that were essential components of promotability. These additional factors and skills are the ones that make the difference.

Promotability

Eichinger labeled these two clusters of competencies as relationships and adaptability. Given all we've discussed in this book about women and their focus on relationships, you might think that this area would be a strength for women managers and leaders.

However, the relationships Eichinger has identified as associated with promotability aren't relationships with one's team or staff—the areas of connection in which women tend to excel. Rather, the relationships that matter are those with *your boss, your peers, and upper management.*

This distinction should not be surprising. Your superiors are the individuals who have the greatest input into promotion decisions. Your peers are often the ones who can speak to your potential and your performance. Yet far too often, women fail to remember this. They spend most of their time and energy focused on their teams and their performance and don't invest enough in the very relationships that will be key to their promotions.

One additional competency is related to these hierarchical relationships: the avoidance or absence of political missteps. A "political misstep" in a company has a lot to do with the culture, the hierarchical structure, and the relational networks that exist across the company. It can be the result of a too-narrow network where you aren't aware of alliances. A colleague once told me about an experience of ranting about an executive to a coworker, only to later discover they were golfing buddies. This kind of information is often shared more informally and is more likely to be accessible to men than women, given their majority status. It pays to be deliberate in forming strong relationships with senior executives who can provide you with political and relational information. Working closely with senior executives helps. Ask to debrief with them after important meetings to understand the rationale behind your boss's approach and what she saw going on in the meeting that influenced her choices. Letting your boss or mentor know you are keenly interested in the interpersonal dynamics of the business will cue her in to share insights when opportunities arise.

Adaptability is Eichinger's second key component linked to promotability. He lists four specific indicators of this skill set:

dealing with uncertainty, learning on the fly, being an open learner, and not being defensive. In many ways, these competencies are quite different from the relational ones. They are, for the most part, behaviors or emotional responses that can be learned and developed over time. However, they can't be learned or developed in isolation. They require opportunities and situations to acquire and demonstrate that you are capable of these skills. A "stretch assignment," an assignment that may be beyond someone's current skill set, is frequently the perfect setting for testing and growing new leadership muscles.

All of these skills require you to act outside your comfort zone—to embrace uncertainty, to learn quickly, to encounter other positions, and be open to opposition. As with many areas of career development, you will need to proactively seek out opportunities to demonstrate adaptability—or at least express your desire for them. Stretch assignments and special projects tend to appear suddenly, and you want your boss and others to have you front of mind when they arise. This is particularly true with respect to assignments that involve considerable travel or international relocation. Unconscious bias can enter in, leading to assumptions about women's willingness to accept such jobs. You want to be sure your boss knows your desires for career opportunities and your openness to relocating.

In addition to gaining the opportunity to "stretch," you may want to engage someone to help you deal with your internal responses to new and challenging situations. A mentor, coach, or counselor can help you process internal responses of fear, anger, defensiveness, and uncertainty. Gaining the skills associated with adaptability first requires the willingness and courage to try something new, to move beyond your comfort zone in order to expand your repertoire. And then, over time, you have the chance to show that you can grow and develop these skills that are essential in more senior roles.

INITIATE CONVERSATIONS

In light of the research on performance and promotability, I want to offer some guidelines for how to carry on conversations with your boss about your performance and career advancement. They address how to plan for, initiate, drive, and orchestrate these discussions. While the content of the two kinds of conversations will differ, the principles are essentially the same.

Own Responsibility

First, assume that you are 100 percent responsible for making these conversations occur. I have often heard clients complain, "I haven't heard from my boss; I don't know what she thinks about . . ." or "My boss hasn't discussed my performance or my career in two years!" When I respond with a series of questions, such as "Are you waiting for a specific answer?" "Does she know that?" "How did you let her know?" it is with the intent that the client begin to take action toward what she needs or wants. It is very easy to become passive in the face of another's authority—waiting for their initiative, their indication, their response. We can succumb to unconscious or unspoken expectations. I want to argue that we need to be advocates for our own needs, and that includes assuming responsibility for critical conversations with our boss.

In *The First 90 Days*, a wonderful handbook for anyone starting a new job, Michael Watkins makes the point repeatedly that the responsibility for action rests on the individual. He also does an excellent job of framing how to have that conversation with a new boss. His five topics—analysis of the business, discussion of resources, expectations of the new boss, preferred style of communication (frequency, mode, topics), and views on development of people—provide a good framework for structured communication about your personal performance and career.

Demonstrate Your Value

While the conversation should be focused on you, the best way to be successful is to link your discussion to the business—how you have contributed to the business recently, what you are tackling at the moment, and what opportunities you see for how you can make an even greater impact. And don't forget, since these conversations are in service of the business, as well as of you and your boss, they are important, even if not urgent.

We live and work in a world where the urgent too often bumps the important. Don't let that happen. Reschedule. Reschedule. Reschedule. Keep trying until the conversation happens; it deserves time and attention, and it *does* matter!

Focus on the Future

Most of the authorized conversations you will have should be driven toward the future—where the business is going, where you are driving results, how you can improve your performance and be ready for increasing roles of responsibility. Eyes on the future will help you orchestrate more effective conversations that carry authority. You might use something like the start, stop, continue tool, where you address what is working well that you want to continue, where something might need to be stopped, and what you might not see that needs to be started. What does your boss see that you are missing? These are the kinds of questions that, when posed and addressed in a performance check-in with your boss, can lead to new insights.

Manage Emotions

There is one more dimension to preparing for an important review, and that is being honest with yourself about your emotional makeup. What things spark a reaction in you? Frustration is often one for women. Do you have command of how you react in high-stakes meetings? I am a crier—I cry at commercials; I cry when I'm happy, sad, or frustrated. I have spent a lifetime trying to manage my tears, with no luck. But I have learned to say, "Please ignore my tears, and let's continue the conversation." As I talk through them, others around me begin to ignore the tears.

Over the years, I have watched women manage their anger or frustration—as it appears in their silence, their expression, the change in speed of their speech, or the ice that seems to descend. I know from watching successful women that they have learned how to manage their emotions effectively—and by that I mean as part of their communication. They have learned to know what they feel and, by experimenting over time with options for channeling those feelings, they have developed a repertoire they can draw on.

There is no magic bullet. Sometimes a client will report how she got through a meeting and a day later is full of regrets over what she didn't say because she just shut down emotionally. Other times, a client will call me to process what took place and see if her emotions were appropriate. I start by saying it isn't the emotions that are or are not appropriate—it's what you do with them. You want to develop a rich toolbox so that you have multiple ways of responding in the moment when emotions are triggered. I am also a big believer in preparation and anticipation. Reducing the element of surprise can give you more control over how you will respond.

Above all, if you can bring a positive attitude to your meetings, about either your performance or your career, your confidence will signal that you are driving questions that are important to the business, and to both your boss and yourself. Conversations about your achievements and your aspirations for the future are an essential part of leadership dialogues. Your attitude and approach can make it easier for your boss to embrace this part of her or his role.

I had a client who was a senior executive in a financial organization who did this very well. Patricia never wavered in her attention to the business or to her responsibilities for developing her team. She took on extra assignments when necessary, served on committees, and mentored talent. She had high standards and held others to them. Her outrage at those who abused the system or others was palpable but never public. She developed a positive approach that brought energy to all that she did and charmed those with whom she worked. When she did have to express displeasure or frustration, her voice was firm and even, but there was no mistaking her meaning. I asked her once about her approach, and she explained that she believed that she made more progress when she approached others with the best of intentions. Her emotional management was outstanding but reminds all of us that how and what we think impacts what we feel, which determines how we act. The best monitor of our emotional behavior is to start with how we frame and think about people and situations.

TYPES OF CONVERSATIONS

In light of the Eichinger research, and in line with traditional HR practices, two conversations with your boss remain essential, no matter how much their format and frequency may change. The first is a frequent check-in on the work that you have done—i.e., your performance. The second is a regular discussion of your career path—where you are now, what your aspirations are, and what it will take to achieve them. These two exchanges are different in content and design but need to be built into your ongoing interactions with your boss.

Insist on Performance Reviews

As I mentioned earlier, performance reviews are in great flux as I write this book. The emphasis now is on feedback in the form of frequent check-ins that address immediate business activity and individual behavior. While this may feel more burdensome to some managers, it can be a great opportunity for you to maximize these conversations. You can address specific areas where you want guidance or draw your manager's attention to activities, accomplishments, or ideas that otherwise may have gone unnoticed. You are in the driver's seat. Include both what is visible and what is not so visible—what was expected and what was beyond expectations or a total surprise because it arose from an unanticipated or unseen need when goals were set. You might consider developing a mechanism to track these data in order to have them readily accessible to discuss in either a scheduled or impromptu check-in. Many apps are useful for this task—and a calendar is as good as most. An honest review covers more than what went well. It's also an opportunity to discuss and review a challenge that might have gone better or a situation that, though resolved, has left some questions. This requires a trusting relationship and can also foster trust.

And, of course, we must always allow time to set our course for the weeks and months ahead. We need to check in on expectations, review challenges and opportunities, and agree to areas of focus for the months ahead. Without this, the check-in is just a performance review broken up into pieces, providing feedback on the past without setting new and agreed-upon goals for the short-term and long-term future. Keep your eye on the future—of the business, of your relationship with your boss, and of your own career development. I am always amazed at how this topic is so easily and frequently dropped from one-on-one meetings between leaders and their bosses. Try not to let it happen to you.

Whatever the guidance is within your organization about these check-in reviews, I exhort you to assume responsibility to see that they happen. Do not wait. Schedule them in advance. Ensure that they occur. Prepare. Make the most of them, and follow up. After all, this is a conversation intended to help you. Don't wait for someone else to make it happen.

Make Time to Discuss Your Career

Today, in addition to the changes in how performance feedback is being constructed and delivered, professionals are also expressing a greater desire for career conversations to happen more often. No longer do employees see themselves staying at the same company for life. They are eager for movement, both up and over. They want to understand what is possible for them within a company and are always looking around at other opportunities. If an employee doesn't feel as if her boss cares about her future, she will start looking elsewhere. The more senior her role, the more frequent the calls from recruiters will be.

Capitalize on the opportunities this shift in approach and attitude has created for you. In addition to having regular performance check-ins, be sure to schedule periodic conversations to discuss your career path. This is when you let your manager know what direction you want to move in the year(s) ahead. Be prepared with specific suggestions for and/or requests about how she can set you up for success.

It never hurts to express gratitude for what your boss has done to support you during the year. Try to identify behaviors that you would like more of, or explain why certain responses are particularly not helpful. These conversations may not be as frequent as those about performance, and they may happen unexpectedly. So being ready when the right moment comes along may be especially important.

In a December 2020 CNBC interview, Dell Technologies senior vice president Najuma Atkinson told a wonderful story. She knew what she brought to her company, she saw a business need, and she knew how she would address it. She also knew that the company welcomed boldness and encouraged employees to share their ideas. At a company event, she approached CEO Michael Dell and pitched him on her idea. He invited her to discuss it further with him, as well as her next steps at the company. "Little did I know that [Dell] was actually paying attention and we were doing some talent reviews," she says. "I took that opportunity to be bold and to ask for what I wanted, and he reciprocated." Her story demonstrates how essential it is to know your own competence and career aspirations, stay attuned to company needs, and have the courage to overcome fear and hesitation to make your offer when the moment arrives. Finally, as I often tell my clients, *comfort is highly overrated.*

In many ways, Atkinson's behavior also lines up with both the adaptability skills and the relationship skills I discussed earlier in this chapter. Atkinson was able and willing to act and learn on the fly, deal with uncertainty, and build relationships with senior executives. She handled her conversations with the CEO in a way that worked—she didn't make a political misstep. Her advice is also aligned with my repeated advice to know what you desire, push out of your comfort zone, and ask for what you want. The marvelous thing is that these actions are all associated with success in promotion.

I imagine if you analyze your time spent in conversation with your boss or other executives over the past year, you will find that the percentage of time you spent on your own performance, development, and advancement was very low. You are not alone. The 2015 Right Management Global Career Conversation Study reports that only one in five female leaders has ongoing career conversations with her manager.

Yet we know these conversations are critical for advancement. So the bottom line is that you can no longer wait for someone else to make them happen. You need to initiate them and be sure they cover both dimensions of performance and promotability. At the core of this is the central tenet of this book: identify what you want, determine how to pursue it, and engage your manager as an ally and sponsor to make it happen. Your initiative and creativity will enable her to use her authority and power on behalf of you and your plan. Cover your successes and strategies for the business, seek out further possibilities to gain financial literacy, have stretch experiences, and build relationships with senior executives. Above all, ask your boss to consciously sponsor you when opportunities arise. Talk to her about you. Together you can create greater value for the company in the future if you are both proactive in the present.

Remember that in addition to the business-related meetings you have with your boss, it's vital to schedule time to review your performance and to discuss development plans for your career. Regardless of what your organization's official HR processes are, you are the one who must make these reviews of the past and plans for the future occur. Track what you have accomplished, and know where you want to go. Be clear and specific about how your boss can help make that happen. Your future success depends upon it.

Chapter 6: Career Conversations

Summary

- In addition to business-related discussions you want to be sure you have regular conversations with your boss about your own career: both to review your performance in an ongoing fashion and to discuss development plans for your career.
- It is important to assume responsibility for these meetings, to link them to the business, and to focus on the future.
- Reviews of performance have morphed into check-ins on more immediate work at hand. Use these to highlight successes and new business opportunities as well as to gain important information and insights on the broader business.
- Recognize that promotions are based on more than stellar performance. They require skill sets that include strong relationships with more senior executives and demonstration of adaptability.

Do the Work

Learn:

- Invest the time in ensuring that you and your boss are aligned on expectations, communication, and deliverables.
- Learn how your boss wants to receive communications, how they want to be included in decisions, and their view of your responsibilities.
- Understand what the key competencies are for promotions as well as performance.

Engage:

- Discuss with your boss and others what kinds of opportunities for stretch assignments there are in your business.
- Discuss how else you might develop the skills of learning on the fly or dealing with uncertainty.

Articulate:

- Create a two- to five-year plan for gaining opportunities to develop the competencies associated with adaptability through stretch assignments or special projects.
- Each quarter determine how to build stronger relationships with one or two senior executives. Include in that plan learning more about their business and how to let them know more about your own career plans.

Do it:

- Design a tracking mechanism that will enable you to be prepared for check-ins with your boss at any time and have the right data and plans available.
- Work on your own career plans so that you are prepared for a conversation with your boss that can outline specific experiences, developmental opportunities, or further training that you wish to undertake to be ready for more responsibility.

CHAPTER 7

——

Manage Money with Authority

When I finished my doctorate in 1994, I knew what I wanted to do. I wanted to change the world by helping women achieve positions of leadership and authority. At that time, however, companies did not have diversity, equity, and inclusion (DEI) positions. If I was to pursue my desire, I would have to start my own consulting firm. Like so many other women with a personal mission, I set out on my own to do the work I felt called to do.

In doing so, I became what author Michael Masterson calls a "reluctant entrepreneur." While keeping my day job (actually, several day jobs of teaching and data analysis), I began offering leadership development programs to women in Fortune 500 companies. As this work took off as Fine Line Consulting, I quickly realized how little I knew about the business side of growing my firm. When I looked around for resources, I discovered that a new women's entrepreneur group was being launched in Boston. It was intended for women who had several years of experience, but I was able to convince the founder, Lois Silverman, to accept me. (I think my novelty as a former nun proved too intriguing for her to say no.)

As time went on, the other members constantly challenged me. "Running a business is about making money," Amy would say. "You need to be more careful about how many people you hire," Ruth would caution. "Sometimes it seems like you hire people to have a community." And all of them were right. Given my background as a nun and an academic, I was very clear on my mission and purpose—and my love of community. I was eager to engage others in joining me. The profit motive, on the other hand, was still new and felt strange. But I quickly learned that if I was to be effective as a coach and consultant to women in Fortune 500 companies, I had to ensure that my own company would survive and thrive by becoming financially literate. I also needed to understand finances for my clients' sake.

LEARN THE LANGUAGE

What helped me most to gain an understanding of monetary matters was to think of finances as a language. I had experience with both the challenges and the importance of learning a language quickly; as a young nun, I had spent six months in Rome with thirteen other women from eleven countries, speaking only French. My order was international, and twice a year, those who were ready to make their final vows came together in Rome, where our headquarters were, for six months of prayer, reflection, and learning.

During that period, I grappled with the frustration of not understanding and not being understood. My French was so limited that I continually had to rely on the help of a translator. I was not able to communicate my ideas or suggestions, so making a difference was hard. Gradually, however, my French improved, and as it did, my ability to participate, contribute, and enjoy the experience increased.

Language competency brings with it a sense of power and the confidence that is at the core of authority. Learning any language requires study, practice, and the courage to speak. The pursuit of financial literacy is no different. Learning the language of finance begins with studying the conceptual frameworks, vocabulary, and essential metrics that form the scaffolding for financial analysis.

There are multiple ways to achieve this goal, both in person and online. An MBA degree or a finance-for-nonfinance-executives program provides the greatest return on investment. The classes, projects, and assignments force you to understand the integration of concepts and their articulation through application. Furthermore, your interactions with faculty and colleagues give you access to a new network of business associates, and the degree demonstrates credibility.

CEMENT YOUR KNOWLEDGE

But a program is only preparation for the work that you must do to grasp the finances of your own organization and industry. While you may have internal and external financial resources to provide financial reporting, you and you alone are ultimately responsible for your organization's financial outcomes. As I learned when I ran my consulting firm, Fine Line, there is no substitute for your own oversight. As with learning a language, you must "use it or lose it."

Many different techniques can help you to "use" your mastery of financial matters. They can be boiled down to three habits: read, ask, and speak.

Read

When it comes to reading, paying daily attention to business news, such as the *Wall Street Journal*, the business section of your local newspaper, and the *Economist* or *Financial Times*, will give you exposure to economic trends and help you to expand your financial vocabulary. Listen to the news or a financial podcast on the way to work (or while you are exercising, walking, or spending the first few minutes in your office). You need to be up to date on business trends for your specific industry and function. Find the analysts and even futurists (Edie Weiner, president and CEO of the Future Hunters, is someone I love to follow) who track what you want and need to know. It is worth taking fifteen to thirty minutes each morning to check out what's happening in your company and industry before you begin the day. You will find ways to use it.

Ask

Your reading and study provide fodder for the second habit: asking. As your curiosity about finances increases, your insights will begin to inform business meetings, discussions, and even casual work conversations. Financial aptitude translates to greater competence in business. Don't choose to defer, and don't choose to be silent during important financial discussions. You don't have to have all the answers; you can bring valuable questions. You can also bring your questions to senior finance executives—including the CFO of your company. This is a simple way to forge stronger relationships with these leaders. It demonstrates your interest in the broader business while giving them a chance to know you, your business, and your career goals better.

An example of how that can work happened for Anna, a general manager and rising star in her company, who did not have an MBA but was not afraid to ask questions. She was super smart and quickly learned how to run a business unit, manage profit and loss, create budgets, and oversee investments. But she realized that she did not understand some of the complexities of corporate financial filings, questions that analysts raised on quarterly earnings calls, or dimensions of what she called "Wall Street speak." She had ambitions to be a Fortune 500 CEO one day and realized these were knowledge gaps she would need to fill. I suggested a finance-for-nonfinance-executives program at one of the premier universities offering the option, but she had a plan that would work better for her. She would ask the CFO if they could meet once a month to discuss financial issues at stake for the company and projections for the organization she ran. In this way, financial concepts would be grounded in a reality that she knew and understood.

The CFO was happy to have these conversations. As they worked their way through annual reports, projected earnings, and the multiple legal documents companies are required to file about everything from executive compensation to investments abroad, Anna quickly became knowledgeable and fluent in the language of business. Several years later, when she joined a public board, she was asked to serve on the compensation committee and felt up to the task.

Equally important, her work with the CFO forged a strong relationship with a key executive in the company, something that might not have happened otherwise. As she rose in the company, the CFO now had confidence in her work and her understanding of the financial dimensions of the business. When Anna presented to the executive team about her business unit or requested funds for a new venture, the CFO asked many questions but was also her key supporter. Three years later, she was recruited to be CEO of a Fortune 1000 company—the first of three she would lead. Today, Anna serves on the boards of three Fortune 500 companies. Her early discipline in gaining financial insights *and* her lessons about how to partner with senior executives have proven profitable throughout her career.

Speak

Anna's story is a great example of how relationships forged within actual work related to the business are often the strongest professional relationships. Like Anna, take the time to meet with finance leaders and demonstrate your desire to understand your company's fiscal challenges and opportunities—and then, once you've asked the questions that you think need asking, don't be afraid to speak up. Throughout the day, incorporate what you read or hear about in the news into what you say at meetings. Forward articles to colleagues and friends inside and outside your company. Post on LinkedIn. Consider hiring someone to track and post relevant articles for you. Seize opportunities when you can demonstrate your fluency in finance. For example, if your team is presenting to the CEO or executive team, you could do the financial overview and have your finance person do the deep dive. You want to demonstrate that you have "financial chops" to those around you—especially to those above you.

THE RUNGS OF FINANCIAL COMPETENCY

Financial proficiency becomes more complex as you move from budgetary oversight to profit-and-loss (P&L) responsibility, and finally to interactions with key external stakeholders, such as your board of directors, investors, and Wall Street. Again, the parallel to learning a language is apt here. While you may be able to travel as a tourist with a knowledge of simple verb tenses, to be fluent in another language, you need more advanced grammar and vocabulary.

Being mindful of this trajectory will ensure that you achieve the developmental milestones necessary for your career ambitions. For some, that means the ability to create, manage, and deliver budgets impeccably. Others want a position that has P&L responsibilities. And for anyone with C-suite aspirations, it means the experience, expertise, and confidence to interact with external, as well as internal, stakeholders. The rungs on this ladder aren't always equally spaced. The move from one level of financial authority to the next is a shift in the nature of responsibility, not just the bottom line. All the more reason to know what your desired destination is so that you can make the most of every opportunity on the journey.

Budgetary Responsibilities

Let's begin by examining the first rung of the financial ladder: budgetary responsibilities. For some, this will be a step on the way, while for others, it will be the primary focus of their career. Regardless of your trajectory, budget management requires that you be adept at creating, tracking, and delivering against budget. It is a core responsibility for any leader, from first line manager to CEO. The breadth, depth, and scope of a budget changes and expands as a leader rises in an organization. Others may handle much of the "nitty-gritty," but the ultimate responsibility remains with the leader.

While all budgets are run according to GAAP (generally accepted accounting principles) methods, a leader's approach to financial resources is often influenced by her own attitudes and experiences with money. Her psychological profile, outlook on money, risk profile, and resourcefulness all contribute to her effectiveness in managing financial resources. Her creativity and generosity, her fear of reproach or making a mistake, her willingness to take risks, her judgment in determining how to allocate resources, and her ability to see changing needs will also contribute to how she manages budgets.

One of my clients, Jan, a vice president at a medical devices company, was high-energy, and her team often teased her that she was getting too far ahead of them. But her ability to get out ahead enabled her to see new needs and the opportunities they presented. Her drive and fearless risk-taking kicked in whenever she saw a chance to compete and win. At the same time, Jan was an absolute stickler for financial honesty. At the end of each quarter, when it was time to report out on their results, she would remind her direct reports that they could not engage in any financial trickery to make things look better than they were—for example, no claiming new accounts that would not begin until the next quarter. Her integrity, matched by her drive to accelerate the use of resources, gained her the respect of all and led to a meteoric rise in her career.

Jan was also unusually creative about how she managed her budget within the rules of the game. She was not afraid to reallocate funds as the year went along if the demands of the business required that she do so. Her message to her team was always, "You propose, and I will find a way to say yes." She would fight for, and usually get, the resources she needed to prototype new instruments for unmet patient needs. Her attitude was that money was the means to success and that her job wasn't to say no to possibilities. She encouraged her team to think big, and she demonstrated how you can and should ask for resources for important business opportunities.

At the opposite extreme from Jan are the micromanagers. I once worked with a company that was two years away from a record-breaking initial public offering (IPO), yet the CEO still expected to personally approve every requisition of more than $25,000. While that may seem like a lot of money, when an annual budget is in the hundreds of millions, $25,000 is not at a level that a CEO should worry about. Micromanaging finances can drain the lifeblood, energy, and passion from the most talented people. Cultivating a balance between oversight, trust, and flexibility is one of the muscle developments that is required before more serious financial acrobatics can be achieved.

Profit and Loss

The second rung of the ladder of financial experience is to gain significant P&L responsibility. Running a business where you are accountable for revenue is usually the most important step to achieve career advancement, yet women often do not recognize this until too late. We are content with doing our jobs well— often very well—but are reluctant to explore or ask for additional responsibilities.

This is different from a budget—no matter how big. When you have P&L responsibility, you are accountable for bringing in revenue—for *making* money for the company. Success here almost always guarantees career advancement. So the key is to be judicious in the roles that you take. Be sure that they are frontline—i.e., leading to revenue and working closer to customers and customer experience. Without these responsibilities, you may have a much harder time achieving an executive role.

Rosemary's experience illustrates how this can happen. She was an IT manager who led a team of engineers in delivering technology solutions internal to her company. She was a hard worker, a proven developer of people, and able to manage crises and the day-to-day grind with equal facility. Her reviews were full of praise for her work and accompanied by bonuses.

After she had been with the company for seven years, a VP position in an IT division came open. Rosemary applied. The process was lengthy. She had many supporters in the organization, since she had always been a team player. But the question that the CIO kept asking was, "Where is her P&L experience?" The budgets Rosemary had managed so carefully and successfully did not demonstrate that she was ready to run an organization where she would need to make strategic decisions about hiring, purchasing, and infrastructure planning. The testaments to her smarts and learning were not enough to sway the CIO. He argued that his responsibility was to ensure that the person promoted or hired into this position had the right experience history. She did not get the job.

Does this story sound familiar? Rosemary had not figured out what her career trajectory would look like. She didn't know what she wanted to do next. Nor had she identified what the necessary notches in her belt were, especially financial expertise, in order for her to be ready when the time came for a promotion.

I have found that many men know exactly what position they want next, and it's usually their boss's job. They factor this into each and every decision and calculate how financial competence and experience can and will contribute to their career advancement.

A successful career requires us to think ahead and know what we want in the future, even if our plans will change multiple times over the years. We must know what we want so we are ready to respond quickly to opportunities when they appear. Good work, whether that is delivering results, developing people, or being "the woman" on every internal initiative, is never enough. You need to become comfortable with finances and develop an internal calculus that enables you to compute your worth to the business and the compensation that should accrue to you.

COMPENSATION

Conversations about money become personal when compensation is at stake. Authorizing yourself to ask for a generous compensation package or a hefty raise is a crucial career skill. Unfortunately, it is often a difficult one for women to develop. I have observed clients who would ask for the sun, the moon, and the stars for their business or their team but fail to make a comparable ask for themselves. They expect that their work will speak for itself. It rarely does alone—or at least it doesn't speak as loudly as it does when it is combined with a clear, deliberate request. Compensation is a metric that demonstrates respect and value. Compensation strengthens your leadership and authority because it tells you how much you matter. Conversations about compensation are necessary *and* an important opportunity to move the needle on gender inequities in pay.

The reality of the gender pay gap exacerbates the challenges women face in discussing compensation. In 2018, the average woman earned eighty-one cents for every dollar men earned. Compared with white men's salaries, white women earned 78.4 percent; Black women, 61.4 percent; Hispanic women, 56.0 percent; and Asian women, 89.4 percent. The cumulative effect of this difference over a career, in both income and advancement, is dramatic. For example, this wage gap will cost college-educated millennial women $1 million over their careers (IWPR, April 10, 2019). As Catalyst, the leading nonprofit working to advance women in business, says, "It's not myth, it's math."

What is the reason for this gap? For a long time, the argument was that women did not ask for a raise as often as men do. In her 2013 book, *Lean In*, Sheryl Sandberg encourages women to be more assertive. Sandberg was criticized for placing too much responsibility on individual women and ignoring the systemic issues that work against their success, but her book did spark a conversation about women's advancement, especially in Silicon Valley. It also led many women to be more proactive in their careers, including asking for greater opportunities and increased compensation.

In a 2018 *Harvard Business Review* piece, "Women Ask for Raises as Often as Men, but Are Less Likely to Get Them," Benjamin Artz, Amanda Goodall, and Andrew J. Oswald reported that women *do* ask for a raise but do not have the same success rate that their male colleagues do. This discrepancy points to systemic issues at play. Regardless, you need to be sure to address your own compensation package throughout your career, especially when you are hired for a new job and, later, when you are given additional responsibilities and have opportunities to ask for a raise.

Negotiate Like a Pro

The most important time to negotiate your salary is when you are being hired, since this will become the foundation of your compensation for years to come. If you have been on the hiring side of a salary negotiation, you know that most managers offer less than what they are prepared to provide, so that they have some room to negotiate. But women can tend to say yes too quickly when offered a position and fail to ask for more compensation. A 2018 survey by global staffing firm Robert Half found that only

34 percent of women tried to negotiate a higher salary during their last job offer.

Negotiating confidently requires preparation. Read up on strategies for salary negotiations. Talk to friends and colleagues who might have valuable insights. Role-play the interview with a coach or friend before you ever talk to an employer. Face your fears head-on. Do your research. Practice how you'll field any salary questions so that you can increase your ability to handle them. Know what you will do if your request is not met. If a company makes you an offer, it's not likely to let you walk away.

Key to your preparation is knowing what your skills are worth. A lot of information about this subject is available online. Payscale.com and Salary.com offer free salary information, and today more people are willing to discuss salary scales than they were in the past. Talk to your male friends—they are often better at negotiating compensation than you may be. Men have been taught how to aggressively go after what they want, whereas women have not, as we've already discussed. They have more experience in discussing compensation among themselves, and in asking bosses, mentors, and friends about what to expect to be paid. Be sure to calculate your years of experience, education, and special training. If you have met others on the team, determine where you fit in terms of experience and expertise. Finally, don't reveal your current salary. A prospective employer will ask you about it, but there is no reason you have to offer that information. (You can give a range.) Instead, ask what the company intends to offer and why.

Similarly, when the time comes to ask for a raise, be specific in your request. Think about, research, and discuss with friends what amount you consider appropriate for a new position or a raise. Don't forget that in any negotiation, a high first request results in a better outcome. Called the anchoring effect, this first step anchors the negotiation that follows. As a colleague of mine often says,

"Unless the amount is high enough to make you feel uncomfortable, it's not high enough."

Remember that a salary negotiation is all about *you* and the value you bring to the business. You are asking for money because of your contributions, past, present, and future, not because you have a mortgage or other financial responsibilities. You must demonstrate to your boss what you have done to *advance the business*. Don't assume she is a mind-reader. Don't assume that she will know what you want or what you deserve. Practice and rehearse the conversation, the way you would for a major business presentation. Include examples of how you have taken on a greater workload, or where you demonstrate next-level competencies and performance. Let your boss know that you take both yourself and the business seriously.

Three stories from my experience as a coach provide insight into how pay negotiations can play out. The first is a lesson I learned from a man named Michael, who worked at a consumer products firm.

Michael reported to Kathleen, the general manager of their organization. An unexpected departure occurred in one of her divisions. While Kathleen conducted the search to fill the position, she needed someone to oversee the group, and she asked Michael to take on this additional responsibility. He responded, "Yes, *and I expect a bonus for it*." When Kathleen asked him how much he had in mind, he said without hesitation, "Forty thousand dollars." This was a significant bonus in the late 1990s, but Kathleen needed someone to oversee the organization, so she said yes. Six months later, after she found and hired a new GM, Michael returned to claim his prize and she dutifully paid out the compensation.

When I heard this story, I was taken aback. I realized that I had never seen a woman make such a request, despite the fact that women had frequently assumed more responsibilities than Michael had. On the other hand, I *have* witnessed women repeatedly handle the responsibilities of two or even three jobs. A friend of mine once joked that she was going to quit and reapply for one of the three positions they would have to create to replace her. Michael taught me the necessity of the ask. When you take on additional responsibility, ask for additional compensation to reflect your heightened workload.

The second compensation story is one I have seen play out repeatedly over the years. Judy was a new client who had recently been promoted to run a large division of a global pharmaceutical company. She was competent and confident, and we got off to a terrific start. Six weeks into her new role, Judy reviewed the compensation history of her team and discovered that one of her direct reports was paid more than she was. He had less experience, less education, fewer years in the industry, and no specific skills that she didn't have. She was shocked and angry.

I asked Judy what she planned to do about it. Together we crafted the conversation she would have with her boss. The focus would be on what *her* compensation package should look like, rather than anger over her direct report's compensation. I urged her to avoid any overt expression of anger. Confrontation and sharing strong emotions often backfire on women. Far better for Judy to present her argument in terms of the business and to convey her confidence that her boss would make things right. She practiced and delivered her message, and her own compensation package was increased appropriately.

The last story I want to share is about negotiating a compensation package at the time of hiring. Serena was recruited by a technology firm that was smaller than her current employer. The new company was pre-IPO, so the components of her compensation were more complex than usual. Nonmonetary issues were important to her too, including membership on the executive team and a change-of-ownership clause in case the company was sold.

Serena did her research, and I reached out to HR executives in my network to gain insights and suggestions on how to structure the deal. When it came time to discuss the job offer, Serena knew what she wanted to ask for, the range to seek, how to structure the complex clauses in the contract, and how to ensure that she had a seat on the executive team. The result was a new job with all that she had asked for and a smooth, respectful hiring process.

Everything is negotiable (even relocation expenses for a pet when you move internationally for work). When women know what they want, they get better at asking for it. Effective negotiations lead to more equitable pay that compounds over time, a feeling of being more valued and respected, and a better, happier foundation for starting at a new company. You can't negotiate unless you ask, however. And to ask, you need to know what you want.

Managing money with authority essentially involves budgets, P&L responsibility, and compensation. You can think of finance as the language of business, and without question the women who are fluent in this language achieve the greatest success. But we should remember that our personal relationship with money can impact how we approach decisions about budgets and spending, so spending time understanding your own history with and attitudes about money, how you manage money and why, and your trust of others is time well spent. Women have made tremendous progress in the field of finance, and in so doing have set the stage for a higher number of female CEOs and board members. But the real challenge lies in helping women early in their careers to understand the importance of financial literacy, seeking out and holding P&L positions, and being courageous and outspoken about compensation. Money matters. The sooner you embrace this fact, the sooner your career can take off.

Chapter 7: Manage Money with Authority

Summary

- Financial literacy is the language of business. Become fluent early in your career.
- Management of a budget, no matter how large, is necessary but not a guarantee of career advancement.
- P&L responsibility—i.e., where you must grow a business—is an essential experience to have early in your career if you aspire to more senior roles in your organization. Seek out positions with P&L responsibility.
- Negotiation is both art and science. Learn the skills and apply them to your own compensation and budgets.

Do the Work

Learn:

- Study finance formally and informally, no matter what your role in your business or organization is.
- Do a personal audit of your own attitudes about and experiences with money. Consider how they influence your approach to your responsibility for finances at work.
- Learn about basic financial responsibilities of management, such as budget planning and oversight. Advance to studying company financial reporting and annual reports, and the role of investors.
- Work with both Finance and HR business partners to understand compensation structures and the financial dimensions of hiring and promotions.

Engage:

- Reach out to your Finance business partner or, if you are in a senior role, to your CFO for mentorship on financial matters. Make this request about more than help as needed—ask these people for regular tutoring on the intricacies of the financial dimensions of your industry and company.

- Discuss with your boss your desire for a role with P&L responsibilities and what you will need to do to be prepared for that role. Renew this ask periodically, when appropriate.
- Pay attention to when P&L positions come open in your company, and apply. The interview process itself will be a valuable learning experience.
- Work closely and regularly with your Finance business partner. Don't wait until a crisis happens.

Articulate:

- Map out a yearly plan for how you will address aspects of your financial development goals.
- Each year, meet with your Finance business partner to identify areas of focus; explore courses that can deepen your knowledge on that topic. Discuss with your boss how these objectives can be part of your developmental goals for the year.

Do it:

- Identify financial goals and objectives for the year and the focus for each quarter.
- Build these into your business plan and developmental goals, and review them with your manager.
- Review these goals with your team too. Explain why they are important and what the team can gain from this focus on greater financial understanding.
- Conduct periodic reviews with your team of the company's quarterly and annual reports as a way to increase everyone's overall financial fluency.
- Pursue volunteer opportunities that include financial components, such as board service for a nonprofit, to gain additional experience.

CHAPTER 8

—

Expand
Your Authority

We all know the importance of broad personal and professional networks when it comes to increasing influence and authority as a leader. Within these networks, it's important to ensure that you have a strong circle of friends and colleagues who recognize your leadership talents and skills and will spontaneously speak up on your behalf, especially in situations where you aren't present. As you grow and nurture your networks, you also want them to be aware of your career aspirations. You want your name to immediately come to mind when an important task force is being formed or a position suddenly comes open. You want your networks to be active advocates for you because they have seen you in action, are cognizant of your past performance, and champion your potential. And, of course, you want to cultivate these relationships both within your company and externally in your industry and community.

You can form these relationships at work, on a team, or through involvement in professional organizations, philanthropic work, or

147

activities related to community or family. Serendipitous encounters can prove invaluable. For example, one of my early clients, Beverly, was a general manager at a manufacturing company. One day, seemingly out of the blue, she received an invitation to join the board of directors of a Fortune 500 company. She had not considered board service at that point in her young career, so at first she wasn't sure how the company had identified her. It turned out that she had been on the local United Way board with someone who also sat on the company's board and had put her name forward. She had been seen, heard, and recognized for her leadership talents.

Serendipitous occasions where your leadership is recognized are wonderful. However, most of the time you will need to be creative, proactive, and persistent in identifying who you want to know you. It is not enough to have achieved career success. Once you are confident in your competence, your experience, and what you have to offer, you must then figure out who could benefit from knowing what you bring to the table. In short, you are giving someone else the opportunity to know who you are at your core: what drives you, your mission and passion in life, and how that informs all that you would like to do in the future.

KNOW WHY YOU ARE AN AUTHORITY

Of course, before you set out to identify who should know you, you must first be clear about your expertise, where you are headed, and the contributions you will make. What are the next chapters of your career? Where would you like to be in five or ten years? As with most journeys, if you lack a sense of the destination, you will find it hard to map out the path for how to get there. Furthermore, another person can't help you until they have a sense of your goals.

In chapter 2, I told the stories of two women who thought it would be many years before they held a top position. When an unexpected opportunity presented itself, they found it difficult to respond. But with encouragement from others, they were each able to reimagine themselves in a senior position, apply for the job, and get hired. But what if they had done that imaginative work beforehand? Their angst about applying might have been a more productive excitement about the fact that what they had envisioned and looked forward to was actually unfolding.

When we engage our imagination, we can see opportunities when they appear and can respond more quickly. I have always loved the story about Michelangelo in which he reportedly claimed he could carve the magnificent marble statue of the *David* because he could see the statue trapped in the stone and his work was to carve it free. If you think about your future as hidden in stone, what do you see? What will it take to carve it out? How much easier it will be for others to help you once you have done that work.

Once you have a clearer picture of where you want to go, you can begin to identify the individuals who may be able to help you get there. Perhaps this includes those who have walked that path before you and/or those who are familiar with the field or industry you wish to work in. What is it that you wish to learn from them? How can they help you? The more specific you are, the greater the chance that they will be able and willing to help. If you have done your homework and narrowed down the who, what, where, when, and why of your ask, you make your chances of success infinitely greater. If your "ask" is specific, others will be more likely to help you make that happen and to open their network to you. And introductions from significant allies are often the key to the connections you are seeking.

In my own career, there have been two moments when knowing exactly what I wanted to accomplish and the mission I had for my career resulted in amazing opportunities. With hindsight, I see how my clarity in knowing what I wanted and letting others know too enabled them to make connections for me that would lead to career- and life-changing results. Neither opportunity would ever have been possible without the introductions that were made on my behalf.

The first moment came shortly after I got my doctorate, while I was launching Fine Line. A friend, Marie, called to say she had been asked to help organize part of a new women's leadership program that was coming to Harvard. She knew of my interest in that area and wondered if I would like to be involved. I jumped at the opportunity and pursued it with passion. By the next summer, I was engaged in the International Women's Forum Fellows Program and would remain so for ten years. Over that period, I began to work with the program's graduates, who brought me into their Fortune 500 companies around the country. Marie's knowledge of my passion and expertise opened the door to this incredible experience.

The second moment came a decade later, after I had moved to California. I was speaking to an insurance agent about securing health insurance as a small business owner. As we discussed my work, she offered to introduce me to another client, who ran a San Jose coaching firm. I became a subcontractor for him, and soon after that, he had a job for me with a woman VP at VMware. This was the beginning of a relationship that would eventually lead to VMware's offering me a position as its VP of organizational and leadership development, the highlight of my professional life.

I share these stories to demonstrate that networking can often be most impactful in moments when we least expect it. Knowing your mission and ensuring that others are fully aware of your competence and passion enable them to make matches with organizations and companies that you might not even be aware of. This is the fruit of regular nurturing of existing and naturally occurring relationships, not an extra burden.

Reframe Your View of Networking

While we all know that many jobs and positions come to us through networks, we can too easily forget the time and effort required to build and maintain a strong network. I'm always a bit dismayed when I see women spending inordinate amounts of time perfecting a presentation or other dimension of their performance but giving little attention to strengthening their networks.

Admittedly, women often have very little discretionary time as they balance work, family, and community responsibilities. When they think about how to spend any limited slice of "free time" they may have, networking events rarely are among their top priorities. Time has become a more cherished asset than money for many of us. (One of my neighbors told me that the nonprofit that she has volunteered with for years is having great difficulty finding younger volunteers. Women are more willing to write a check than to become involved in fundraising or other activities that require a major time commitment.)

I once asked several women who are exceptional networkers about their secrets to success. Marsha told me, "You have to change your mindset. Instead of saying 'I *should* go' or 'I have to go,' be curious about who might be there. Ask yourself, *Is there* one *person I would like to meet or reconnect with who is on the guest list?*" Following Marsha's advice, I altered my approach to the meetings I attended. Before an event, I now review the list of attendees and try to identify one or more individuals I would like to meet or reconnect with. I like to get there early, which then makes it easier to find the person I'm looking for when she arrives. But the best part of this is that I now have a mission and a purpose while also being open to the unexpected magic that can occur in a group of smart, talented women.

Louise, who runs a blog on women in technology, is always looking for interesting people to interview. When I asked her about her approach to networking events, she explained, "I go to the meeting with a few questions that are related to the topic of the event and use them to engage with perfect strangers. When I find someone interesting, I pursue the conversation by asking more about their background and work. If they're not interested in chatting, I move on to the next person." She has found that acting like a reporter has made networking events both more interesting and more enjoyable. She feels a sense of agency. And she often comes away with guest speakers for her blog. Acting like a reporter is an approach that I have also tried, with great success and fun results.

Consuela told me that she uses networking opportunities to practice talking about the new business she is launching. She finds that trying out her "pitch" or "elevator speech" with real people is much more effective than working on it alone. "It pushes me out of my comfort zone and gives me immediate feedback about real-time ideas. It has also helped me make valuable contacts." I remembered her advice when I started working on this book and tried different "pitches" to see which one was most effective in drumming up interest. The practice increased my confidence and spread the word about the book in advance of its publication. I also became much more eager to attend networking events.

Karen Wickre, in *Taking the Work Out of Networking*, offers yet another approach: "if you can approach networking based on what you can give someone else, it lessens the awkwardness you may feel about what you need." If you listen to others as they talk, you may hear things that they are struggling with, information they need, or something you can offer to get back to them with. It can be an article, a connection, a resource. Whatever it is, you will have a follow-up exchange and each of you will feel better for it. Once you are connected with this person, you should encourage what Wickre calls the "loose-touch habit," where you stay in contact by forwarding information that is germane to what you discussed. Networking events can be contact-rich opportunities if you have a plan, identify what success will look like, work the plan, and follow up. Get there early, move around, and be generous, focusing on others.

No matter what approach you take, the key is to create your own sense of agency. Instead of feeling like you *should* attend an event, I suggest that you approach it with an attitude of *curiosity*. Instead of focusing on the whole crowd, identify *one strategic person* whom you will seek out. Set out with a mission, instead of wandering around, feeling lost. Full of this energy of purpose, curiosity, and expectation, you will see the participants in a different light.

Cumulatively, this suddenly sounds different from the traditional approach to events. It changes your thoughts and feelings and leads to a new outcome. Fully engage, and I predict that your new energy will make you a beacon to others who will want to meet *you*!

Take It Online

Much of what I have written assumes that we will be able to meet again in person once the pandemic is under control, hopefully soon. But this time of virtual connections has also offered some new and unexpected opportunities. The virtual world has made it possible to attend local, national, and even global events that previously would have been impossible to take part in. These chances to learn, to meet, and to connect have been amazing. Many who would otherwise be on the speaker circuit and been hard to reach or expensive to hear can suddenly be seen and heard from the comfort of your office. Even more important, you can reach out afterward and contact them. I have made some unexpected and wonderful connections by following up after programs.

I have also observed that our virtual world is a new experience for many of the presenters as well. They appreciate your feedback and are grateful for the follow-up. They miss the crowd waiting to talk to them after an event. We are all in this together, and the opportunities for new ways to connect are very real.

BE MEMORABLE

The key to expanding your authority is to consider how you will become memorable. We know that first impressions matter, as does perceived expertise. And in today's world, repetition of appearance is also required to break through and make a lasting impression. We must be deliberate in how we present ourselves to the world, invest in crafting introductions and content that will matter to the audience we want to meet, and embrace this outreach as an opportunity, not a burden. We will become memorable not just for what we know but for how we make others feel about getting to know us.

Introductions Matter

The key to introductions is to make yourself memorable. We all know that we need an elevator speech that captures who we are and what we are about. In 2017, I met Joanna Bloor, CEO of The Amplify Lab, who helps people reframe how we think about introductions. Her advice is to "go beyond your job title." When people ask you, "What do you do?" use their question as an opportunity to tell them about what you want to be known for. Tell them the impact that you want to have on others and the world. When I tried this, it worked. I found it easy to speak about my desire to accelerate the advancement of women. When I tried to answer Bloor's question, "What is at the heart of what you do for others?" I knew what to say right away: "I want to change the world one woman at a time." When she asked, "What is the specific problem you solve, and how is your approach unique?" I finally had a chance to change my old introduction, "I am an executive coach" (which so many people today are), to "I enable women to name and claim their desire to lead, and accelerate their journey to roles of authority and influence." Bloor pushed me to articulate what matters most to me and then to invite others to learn more about this important part of my life.

Bloor's encouragement and reframing enable us to craft introductions that open a conversation, instead of shutting it down. And we feel so much more powerful because the words are coming from our core and capture our whole life's mission and vision. Her approach focuses on what matters most to you, rather than on describing a job title.

Most women I have known converse more readily about their passions than they do about themselves. Putting passion out there for all to see enables others to connect, which is the ultimate goal of networking—to identify where there is synergy to build on. Mastery of your introduction is crucial to expand your network and to enable others to know who you are, what you are passionate about, and why they should want to know more about you. Crafting an introduction that resonates will change how you feel about networking opportunities to share your story with others.

Be a Thought Leader

Introductions, no matter how well crafted, are at most a few minutes. You also want to think about what follows an introduction. You want to be sure you are attentive to the other person. Your genuine curiosity about what they are saying and who they are is the best place to start building the conversation. You want the other person to feel heard. At the same time, this is your opportunity to articulate your value proposition, expertise, or thought leadership in a way that relates to any thorny problem she has on her plate. Many ways to communicate value to others exist; one is as a thought leader.

With the advent of social media, anyone can create a digital platform and become well known. However, to be an effective thought leader, you need to be specific about your area of expertise and the audience you serve. You don't want to be all things to all people. Not only is that too grandiose, but it is impossible to achieve. You should know who your specific audience is and what the adjacencies might be.

Denise Brosseau, CEO of Thought Leadership Lab, in her book *Ready to Be a Thought Leader?*, describes thought leadership as an offering that you bring to others when you have been able to codify your passion enough to share it. Being a thought leader is a way to be found in order to be of service. Often thought leaders are people who have distilled ideas into a book, but today they can also be found via online resources like LinkedIn Learning courses.

Thought leadership sets you apart because of your unique value proposition and how you bring this value to others. To become a thought leader, you must move beyond a passion and vision for your work. You must move beyond top performance and even high visibility. You must carve out a platform where you can make your vision, your passion, and your ideas accessible to others in a way that works for them. A thought leader makes meaning out of experience, expertise, and the needs of the moment.

Our inspirations evolve as we do. Today, the environmental activist Greta Thunberg—so young and yet so clear, and so willing to become a leader in the face of great odds—motivates me, as does Malala Yousafzai, who turned a horrific near-death experience into fighting for girls' and women's rights. And all the unknown women around the world who run small and large organizations to help women advance. And all the women and men who work within companies and are incorporating DEI principles and practices into how they do business.

When I began my career in 1995, I was told that I was crazy to focus only on women. By sticking to my vision and passion, I have been able to integrate academic expertise, entrepreneurial experience, and corporate leadership—all focused on women. My dedication to this mission, and the experience I have accumulated over the years, have made me a thought leader in my field.

Be Discoverable and Top of Mind

Becoming known as a thought leader means that others must be able to find you. In their book, *Authority Marketing*, Adam Witty and Rusty Shelton suggest you do a personal audit of how you appear online and how easy or difficult it may be for someone to find you. Today more than ever, social media is the primary way to show the world who we are and what we do. Personal references and recommendations still matter, but typically the first way someone learns about us is by googling us. While our own participation and interest in the social media world may range from very active to indifferent, we can't ignore the fact that we must and do appear online. Moreover, we must be sure that how we appear in our online accounts is consistent with who we are. Our online presence communicates to others what we do and what we are about before we have a chance to explain that personally. A poor or missing online presence is a message in itself.

When I stopped working at VMware, I realized that while I considered myself a thought leader in my field, I was not findable. My social media presence was limited, and my website needed serious revision. As I worked on this book, I undertook a social media audit to see what someone else finds when they search for me. It wasn't bad, but it wasn't what I wanted it to be. It took serious effort and help from others to uplevel my presence online. But it was worth it.

Become a Content Creator

Increasingly, people are finding ways to gain authority as experts through writing and/or posting content online. Writing a book is also a great way to accomplish this goal. Today, on social media platforms like LinkedIn, Medium, Facebook, Twitter and ever newer ones, people are choosing to put forward their ideas through posts, rather than navigating the complexities of the publishing industry. This is certainly a way of expanding your authority.

We all have a different relationship with social media, depending on our time, our interests, and our purpose. Like many, I belong to groups on Facebook and follow many people and topics on LinkedIn. I have also worked to become engaged in conversations of interest and importance to me and my clients. I have studied different ways in which people post—some basically post ads for their services; others share valuable information about events. I also love seeing congratulatory posts when a breakthrough hire happens or someone receives an award that I might not otherwise have known about. I am particularly grateful for those who are true curators of information, like Dr. Marianne Cooper, a senior research associate at Stanford University. She posts from a broad range of sources on women, work, and diversity and offers a brief note about why each post is worth reading. She makes me smarter and more connected, and I am always grateful.

Another regular post comes from Brooke Warner, publisher of She Writes Press, who shares motivating and encouraging comments about the writing process. She will often pose a question to encourage a conversation among her audience. Here, I find I often pause to consider her question or prompt and to think more seriously about my own writing. I am grateful to be moved forward in my thinking on a new topic. I also appreciate her invitation to respond. Writing is a solitary affair, and Brooke's Facebook and LinkedIn posts extend a sense of community.

One way to get yourself out there is to get involved in today's world of podcasts, which have an endless need for interesting experts to interview. If participating in an interview is easier for you than writing a piece to post, this may be the right path to pursue. (Note: It is always a good idea to follow a podcast before you offer to be a guest—both to be sure it is a good match and to have a better sense of the host when you reach out.)

Another path to consider is becoming an authority available to reporters working on deadline. One great site to check out is HelpAReporter.com, where you can sign up to receive twice-daily requests from reporters with specifics about whom they would like to speak with. Despite the range, from economics to travel to family life, you will quickly get a sense of which categories fit your profile. It's interesting to see what reporters are writing about; every so often, I get a request that I forward to a client who is the perfect resource for the topic. For example, in 2020, a reporter wanted to interview senior marketing or operations managers on how they ensure their teams' work is impactful. One of my clients fit that profile, and it was a great opportunity for her to get some press coverage. You have to be willing to take the call without the kind of preparation most of us like. This is a form of the adaptability we discussed earlier as a competency for promotability. We may want to be perfectly ready for a media call, but if we can adjust our comfort level, we might gain more coverage.

Dozens of other platforms where you can present your content are available as well: YouTube, TED Talks, Twitter, etc. Find the ones that will work for you. Create the platforms you need or develop a plan to be the guest on others' platforms; either approach will expand your visibility and authority. Be creative, patient, and, above all, persistent.

Extending your authority beyond your immediate contacts takes time and effort, whether in person or virtually, but the rewards will be worth the investment. The key is how you frame your approach, both in person and in online connections. You want to remember that attitudes of curiosity and generosity will serve you well. Above all, networking, engagement in social media, and finding ways to be a source for others can be rewarding both personally and in terms of your career advancement. Remember these three steps: 1) Know where you are headed; 2) identify who can help you get there; and 3) determine how they can get to know you. In other words, do for yourself what you most likely are doing already for so many others as a mentor, confidant, and friend.

Chapter 8: Expand Your Authority Externally

Summary

- To continue to grow your career, you must expand your authority beyond your organization and personal contacts.
- You must be clear about your career goals and communicate that to others before they can help you advance.
- Consider how you can become more discoverable or a thought leader in your field.
- The social media space offers multiple opportunities to name and claim your authority.

Do the Work

Learn:

- Reach out to and reconnect with your broader circle of friends and colleagues who already recognize your talents as a leader and can speak on your behalf when you are not present.
- Identify who *should* know you in your field but doesn't. This includes people who are in positions of influence from which they could positively impact your career if they knew you.
- Consider how you could become a thought leader in your own field. Determine how you can carve out a platform to make your ideas accessible to others.
- Consider the extensive networks of women that can be found on social media and the networks of male allies that are emerging. Determine where you could contribute and participate online.
- If you are still trying to figure out how to have a social

media presence, look at how people you admire are doing it, but also pay attention to the younger generation, who have mastered this medium. They have much to offer and teach.

Engage:
- Your approach to building these networks and making these contacts, whether in person or online, should reflect who you are and your values and should take into account how you want the other person to feel.
- When attending live networking events, identify a purpose before you go. This could be a person you want to meet or an introduction you want to make. But be clear why you are there, and have a task to accomplish. This will give you energy and focus.
- Be clear on what you have to offer others. What are you passionate about? What do you bring to others? Craft a new introduction, rather than your current job description, to convey that.
- Above all, be interested in others, and you will in turn be interesting to them.
- Choose a platform where you can begin to present thought-leadership ideas.
- Seek to be of service, and where you can make connections.

Articulate:
- In your journal, write out your plan for where you want to be in twelve to eighteen months. Who needs to know you to help make that happen? Map out a list of who you want to meet, and figure out how and when.
- Turn the list into specific goals and objectives. Identify steps you need to take to reach the individuals you believe are important to your career path.
- Spell out what your goal is, schedule your deliverables,

and consider establishing an accountability system with a friend or colleagues.

- Remember that building a network is like training for a marathon—slow but deliberate.

Do it:

- Take the specific goals and map them out across a year. Be realistic but consistent. Determine how much time—perhaps one to two hours dedicated every week—will lead to considerable progress.
- Track contacts you've made and how your social network is expanding. Pay attention to how it is bringing you closer to the individuals you identified as key to your career.
- Notice new opportunities that are arising. Once per quarter, review your plan and make changes where appropriate and/or necessary.
- Enjoy the expanded authority.

Conclusion

This book began its life, as you may recall from the introduction, many years ago in a Harvard classroom on a cold December night full of holiday glow and the buzz of semester's end. I was still a nun in my second year of a doctoral program studying women's psychological development. That final night of a course on leadership at the Harvard Kennedy School triggered questions about women's experience in formal roles of authority. They would define my thirty-year career as a researcher, entrepreneur, corporate executive, and executive coach and would ultimately result in this book.

I have always felt confident that women are strong and effective leaders in even the most challenging of circumstances. My questions have revolved around their personal experience of exercising leadership in formal roles of authority. My work with women executives over the years offered me the insights that gave life to the research and theories I had studied.

In stark contrast with that scintillating winter's night of conversation in a crowded classroom, I completed *Lead* in solitude and isolation during the COVID-19 pandemic. My husband died the week before we went into lockdown. As I sat alone each evening after working on the manuscript all day, I watched the country and the world confront daunting questions about the exercise of authority and its impact on the lives of millions. As the virus ravaged the United States, women exercised their authority in powerful ways in other countries around the world. Considerable media coverage has been devoted to how the countries with women leaders—Katrín Jakobsdóttir (Iceland), Tsai Ing-wen (Taiwan), Angela Merkel (Germany), Jacinda Ardern (New Zealand), Sanna Marin (Finland), Mette Frederiksen (Denmark), and Erna Solberg (Norway)—fared much better than male-led countries during the crisis. Many have wondered what it was about these women's leadership that enabled them to lead their very diverse countries. I wasn't surprised—I had always believed that women could and would lead with compassion and drive effectively toward important goals.

Over the same year, we saw teenage climate activist Greta Thunberg speak truth to power, chastening world leaders for not taking climate change seriously. We watched the Black Lives Matter movement mobilize millions to fight for racial justice—a movement founded by three women: Alicia Garza, Patrisse Cullors, and Opal Tometi. And we witnessed Kamala Harris, the first Black woman and first South Asian woman to be sworn in as vice president of the United States of America. In 2020, women rose to enormous challenges, claimed their authority, and led. As I watched all this happening, I found myself wondering over and over what it would be like if we could expand women's authority roles in government, business, medicine, law, and every other field. I believe that more women in positions of power will help us all create a world with greater justice, equality, and care for the weakest among us. This is the vision that has driven my life, my work, and this book. My hope is that the book will offer women encouragement and inspiration.

Lead examines how *you* claim *your* authority when you are in charge. It is built on the premise that claiming your authority and your power begins from the inside out. Don't count on your role or your title for permission. Know what matters to you, what your mission is, and what drives you. This is where your source of power and authority will come from—even when external conditions differ or change.

Your authority is amplified by how you communicate and connect with others and is impacted by your context. But the starting point is you. Our inner self is where we uncover our deepest desires, our driving mission, what we want to do in life, who we want to be. I am always amazed at how often women struggle to answer the question, "What do you want?" But this is where authority begins. You must begin by knowing above all what you want for your life and for your career.

We must also be aware that at our core are dialogues that we carry on with ourselves that impact how we feel and the actions we take. As we discussed in chapters 2 and 3, cognitive psychology has shown us that when we change how we frame our thoughts, when we alter our inner dialogues, we can change their impact on our emotional state and free ourselves to act differently. Women often experience a full symphony of discordant voices: the inner critic, fear of failure, impostor syndrome, split vision, and unspoken expectations that are toxic and disabling. I encourage you to use the suggestions in this book to recognize these voices so that you can manage them. Tune your ear to them the way an orchestra conductor tunes in to different instruments. We cannot rid ourselves of these voices, but we can turn down their volume or counter them with an alternative script. Several times in the book, I have mentioned creating a mantra—something to say to yourself. A mantra can help as a counterforce. Write down a few mantras on Post-its so that they are ready to help you reframe the conversation when those negative voices begin to play.

Once we know what we want, once we are clear on our desires, our mission, our vision, we need to turn our attention to our communication. Throughout this book, I have placed emphasis on how women are seen and heard by others. Women have been "dinged" in the past for not having executive presence, without always knowing what that means. You need to know what it means in your culture. You need to know what effective communication, in its written, virtual, and in-person forms, looks and sounds like. And you need to take steps to ensure that you are an excellent communicator in all media. We all need to push ourselves out of our comfort zone to get training and practice in presenting, to address how we speak and how we use our voice, and to understand how others hear us. This era of Zoom calls has given all of us a chance to examine these details more closely. Use these virtual encounters to see how you come across. Notice your expressions; pay attention to your impact on others. When calls are recorded, you can return to them and listen to how you sound. Have you ever noticed how successful women have wonderful, resonant voices? My guess is that they worked to make that happen. An investment in presentation-skills training, focusing especially on how your voice comes across, will be invaluable.

But the real work of leadership and authority occurs in the context of relationships. The challenges today's leaders face are enormous. We know from experience and from research that women have the skill most needed in leaders today: emotional intelligence. What I have tried to address in this book is what women have not always paid enough attention to: the relationships that impact their own success and career trajectory. Women tend to keep their attention focused "down" on the people for whom they are responsible. You need to make a deliberate effort to "look up and out" at your peers, at other parts of the company, at senior leaders, and at outside influencers. You want to strengthen those relationships, find ways to interact more regularly, collaborate, check in, and be known by those at and above your level. These are the relationships that will open up opportunities for stretch assignments, promotions, and career advancement. These are the relationships that will provide vital information about your organization and your company as a whole. And these are the individuals who can become allies. You must recognize that building relationships is part of your job. It is not a "nice" thing to have or to do. It is an essential component of your role as a woman leader in a role of authority.

I also want to encourage women to do for themselves what they do so well for others: pursue the conversations they need to have to ensure that their careers are on track. I have seen women invest time, energy, and political capital in the development and advancement of people on their teams. They do performance reviews and regular check-ins to confirm that others are ready for promotions. Yet they frequently do not receive the same treatment from their bosses. I have suggested active pursuit of two conversations to make sure you are on track: one about performance and one about career advancement. Don't wait. Take the initiative. Make it happen.

I want to underscore once again the importance of building relationships with other women, especially as you rise in an organization. The higher you get in most organizations, the fewer women you will find. For all the progress we have made, there remain cultural influences that can make it hard for women in senior roles to feel comfortable supporting each other. I have often observed subtle, and not so subtle, ways in which two women on a senior team can be pitted against each other through comparisons, or how men on the team view and treat them. I have also seen senior women reluctant to be identified with other senior women, for fear that such a connection would detract from how they are seen as business executives. We need to avoid letting ourselves be afraid or even hesitant about building bonds with other women executives. We need to bring more women onto these teams, not compete with or resist each other.

We also need to reach out across differences, especially differences of race. Our country is at a moment of moral reckoning with respect to how racism is built into the fabric of our institutions. Those of us who have benefited from white privilege have much work to do. We need to educate ourselves, learn how to speak up and intervene at work and in our communities, and advocate for women of color. Most important, we have to model that we can be allies. Working together, white women and women of color can push for systemic and cultural change that will lead to greater inclusivity, diversity, and equity across the board.

I find great hope for the future in the way I'm seeing women forge bonds outside the workplace today. These bonds have led to women's stronger support of one another professionally, as well as personally, and over time have led individuals to become more explicit in their commitment to advocacy on behalf of all women. One of the organizations that I belong to in the Bay Area is How Women Lead, founded by Julie Abrams. It runs a global leadership program for women and a venture capital fund for women investors and startups with a commitment to invest in companies founded by women of color. Its goal is to be a catalyst for change and make a difference for all women.

How Women Lead does something very simple that is both thrilling and impactful. At the beginning of every meeting, someone reads aloud the organization's credo:

1) Be fierce advocates for each other.
2) Say yes to helping each other.
3) Reinforce her voice.
4) Be unabashedly visible.

Abrams has explained that the reason for this credo is to counter the systems women have grown up in that have eroded our trust in one another. The commitment creates a new way of being together—a safe space where everyone can let down their guard and be what we really want to be inside: loving, supportive advocates and friends. I have this credo on a poster in my office as a reminder of what I need to do as a coach, a writer, and a woman leader. It is also a reminder of the progress women have made since a time when they felt as if few resources or opportunities existed for them and believed that they needed to be more competitive to succeed.

It is essential to remember that we live and work and form relationships within systems. Early in my life as a Catholic nun, I saw the impact that the patriarchy of the Catholic Church could and did have on religious women throughout the world. Systems have power and authority that we must recognize and understand. We must learn how to use our authority to activate systemic levers for change. Power structures are maintained by those who benefit from them. I have always fought against sexism but today recognize that as a white, heterosexual, able-bodied woman, I must expand my fight for justice and equality. I must use the power that comes from my privilege to work on behalf of all women, just as I have asked men to work on behalf of women. And I must realize that doing so will take patience and perseverance when change is not immediately obvious.

We must be organizationally astute, both as individuals and collectively, as we try to harness the moment of goodwill we see in the corporate sector. Many new efforts and forms of energy are arising in the DEI space. We must use our power and authority to hold our organizations accountable for goals and commitments that they make. We must ensure that they really address inclusion, not just diversity, and that the inclusion is equitable. We also have individual power to provide support, mentoring, and advocacy. As we recognize our own authority, we will see how much more influence we have.

We have so much to do on every front for the world's future and for future generations: climate change, education, racial equity, health care. We must all ask ourselves how and where we will name and claim our authority and how we will use that authority to make a meaningful difference. We can do it if we do it together. And do it we must. The world, the planet, our children, and our loved ones all need us to step up.

Each chapter in this book has offered suggestions on how you can begin your own call to action, how to LEAD: to learn, to engage others, to articulate a plan, and to do it. Choose a place to begin. Map out a plan. Find an accountability partner. Do it. Do it together. I have great hope that if we join forces across our differences, we will discover new ways to work together on issues that are critical to all of us. The world needs us now more than ever. Let's claim our authority. Let's lead well.

Index

Index

Index

Index

Index

Index

Acknowledgments

—

Writing a book is challenging but finding a publisher today is a daunting task. I was truly blessed when I found Brooke Warner and She Writes Press. Brooke's guidance as both a writing coach and a publisher enabled me to bring vision and voice to paper. The staff of She Writes Press offered clear and steady guidance throughout the process. In particular, Krissa Lagos provided essential developmental editing, Shannon Green was a steady and patient project manager, and Gerilyn Atteberry designed the wonderful cover. The She Writes Press authors have been a wonderful community of support throughout the journey to publication.

If it takes a village to raise a child, it took a team to bring this book into the world: Amy Whitaker has provided social media expertise, Emi Battaglia has garnered publicity, Dan Blank has been both coach and consultant on marketing, and Alison Macondray and Matthew Clark have turned the book into a story that is ready to share with audiences of every size. Each one has added much joy to the process.

Throughout the journey, I have had generous and supportive readers at every step. My longstanding writing group, Heidi Hackford, Beth Duff-Brown, and Anmol Mahal, read monthly chapters of an earlier memoir version of this book. Heidi has continued her support with repeated manuscript reviews and weekly check-ins. Liz Tucker provided a detailed review of the book at a critical juncture. Alison Wynn provided a response to the book that was both scholarly and practical. Denise Brosseau offered key insights into use of social media and introductions that proved invaluable.

Rashmi Gupta, Jessica Amortegui, and Laura Ortman were unanimous on an earlier chapter that needed to be completely changed. Nancy Kehoe rscj and Gail O'Donnell rscj read for clarity about my life as a nun. Amy Bermar brought her expertise as a former reporter and PR executive to our discussions.

Deborah Plousha-Moore and Yvette Hollingsworth Clark have engaged with me around race and intersectionality in the workplace. Their generosity of time, energy, and perspective has enriched my life and—I hope—made the book more responsive to the current reality, which demands greater inclusivity.

I have called on numerous friends and colleagues to read specific chapters. Their insights into the content was invaluable and led to major revisions in several cases. These women I consider my greatest treasures: Theresa Kushner, Marian Davis, Denise Brosseau, Barbara Adachi, Deborah Plousha-Moore, Yvette Hollingsworth Clark, Amy Bermar, Cathy Saunders, Beverly Slade. I was helped by Ellen Weiss, Laura Heisman, Nancy Glaser, and Valerie Corradini in brainstorming book titles. Anne Anderson, Barbara Creed, June Levin, Nicola Acutt, Theresa Kushner, Marian Davis provided final reviews of the text.

Gratitude

———

In addition to those who have contributed to the completion of this book, the insights and experiences within are the fruits of many villages of women who have provided the emotional, intellectual, and inspirational support that enabled me to write *Lead*. To all of them I feel an enormous sense of gratitude. My family was where I first learned the importance of caring for others and the value of community. The Religious of the Sacred Heart, my community as a nun, showed me what having one heart and one spirit can mean. Here I also learned how women of different personalities and cultural backgrounds can hold authority with grace and power within patriarchal systems.

There are several women who have played a pivotal role in my life. Carol Gilligan's writing and teaching changed my life and set me on the course to be a writer. Her courage, compassion, and curiosity inspired me to pursue my own real questions and create a career that has made a difference for other women.

Cynthia Loker, Jan Schubert, Beth Kelley, and others on the Fine Line Consulting team helped me turn theory into practice and touch the lives of hundreds of women in companies across the country. Betty Steiger, a former executive at Xerox and a woman who I believe would have been a CEO in another moment in time, was my mentor both professionally and personally. She and her husband, Don, became my West Coast parents and provided love, encouragement, and any help I needed during my first decade in California.

Betsy Sutter, Chief People Officer at VMware, gave me the opportunity to cross over from consultant/coach to corporate executive when she hired me as VP of Leadership and Organizational Development. This opportunity to work at a technology company at its critical stage of growth was thrilling, and a marvelous complement to my years of work as an outside consultant. The chance to launch the VMwomen's Initiative with Theresa Kushner and executives from across the company was the experience of a lifetime. This work demonstrated how to link diversity and inclusion to business goals and objectives and establish metrics for accountability.

My life has been deeply touched by the clients and mentees I have had the privilege to know and accompany on their journeys. I have learned so much from each of you, and it has been a great joy to watch you discern, decide, and take action on behalf of yourself and your organizations. You are a big part of the story, the insights and the wisdom contained within. To each of you, my deepest gratitude.

My understanding of women's experience has been informed by my participation in The International Women's Forum, a part of my life for twenty-five years. The opportunity to teach in their Fellows program for ten years and to meet so many future women leaders was pivotal. The members of the IWF Forum in Northern California have provided friendship and community for many years. More recently, Barbara Adachi and the members of the Champions of Racial Equality have given me the opportunity to work collaboratively for racial equality while completing *Lead*.

My friends of a lifetime—Terry Healy, Annette La Greca, Nora Kurkul, Nancy Kehoe rscj, Gail O'Donnell rscj, Amy Bermar, Deborah Tindale, Cathy Saunders, and Lynette Brohm—have provided love, support, and friendship that has been as faithful as the dawn. You have kept me grounded, lifted me up when I was down, and reminded me that I was never alone and always loved.

And finally, to the man in my life who brought me more happiness than I had imagined was possible and always kept me laughing, my beloved husband, Richard. His pride and delight in my accomplishments was always something that amazed me. His love supported me as I wrote this book and while he passed before it was finished, I know that somehow, somewhere, he is smiling at its completion.

About the Author

Photo credit: David Gauger

Ellen Snee has been at the forefront of women's leadership for more than twenty-five years. Dr. Snee brings strategy, research, and executive experience to global companies and their top female talent.

Her original research at Harvard University on women's experience in roles of authority formed the foundation of her work with Fortune 500 companies such as Cisco, Goodyear, Marriott, Pfizer, and Schwab. Later, as Global VP of Leadership Development at VMware, she launched its business initiative, VMwomen, to attract, develop, advance, and retain talented women.

She continues to coach and advise women leaders and executives worldwide, and frequently speaks at conferences.

SELECTED TITLES FROM SHE WRITES PRESS

She Writes Press is an independent publishing company founded to serve women writers everywhere. Visit us at www.shewritespress.com.

Drop In: Lead with Deeper Presence and Courage by Sara Harvey Yao. $14.95, 978-1-63152-161-4. A compelling explanation about why being present is so challenging and how leaders can access clarity, connection, and courage in the midst of their chaotic lives, inside and outside of work.

People Leadership: 30 Proven Strategies to Ensure Your Team's Success by Gina Folk. $24.95, 978-1-63152-915-3. Longtime manager Gina Folk provides thirty effective ways for any individual managing or supervising others to reignite their team and become a successful—and beloved—people leader.

The Business of Being: Soul Purpose In and Out of the Workplace by Laurie Buchanan, PhD. $16.95, 978-1-63152-395-3. From a business plan and metrics to mission and goals with everything between—investors, clients and customers, marketing strategies, and goodwill development—this book clearly maps how to create personal transformation at the intersection of business and spirituality.

The Thriver's Edge: Seven Keys to Transform the Way You Live, Love, and Lead by Donna Stoneham. $16.95, 978-1-63152-980-1. A "coach in a book" from master executive coach and leadership expert Dr. Donna Stoneham, *The Thriver's Edge* outlines a practical road map to breaking free of the barriers keeping you from being everything you're capable of being.

This Way Up: Seven Tools for Unleashing Your Creative Self and Transforming Your Life by Patti Clark. $16.95, 978-1-63152-028-0. A story of healing for women who yearn to lead a fuller life, accompanied by a workbook designed to help readers work through personal challenges, discover new inspiration, and harness their creative power.

She Is Me: How Women Will Save the World by Lori Sokol, PhD. $16.95, 978-1-63152-715-9. Through interviews with women including Gloria Steinem, Billie Jean King, and Nobel Peace Prize recipient Leymah Gbowee, Sokol demonstrates how many of the traits thought to be typical of women—traits long considered to be soft and weak in our patriarchal culture—are actually proving more effective in transforming lives, securing our planet, and saving the world.